Moses Mashwahla Moreroa

SUCCESS
COMES IN SEVEN PIECES

SEVEN
PRACTICAL STRATEGIES TO TURN YOUR CHALLENGES
Upside Down

INFORMATION GIANTS *Publishers*

Information Giants Publishers

Visit our website at www.informationgiants.co.za

Information Giants Publishers name and logo are registered trademarks of the Information Giants (Pty) Ltd.

Printed in South Africa

ISBN: 9 7 8 – 0 – 6 2 0 – 7 6 3 7 3 – 8
First Edition, Second Impression February 2018

Cover and Interior Design
Information Giants (Pty) Ltd

Editors
Tom Learmont
Metji Makgoba

This book is dedicated to all the unrewarded hard workers, young and old, and poor and rich, who continue to beat all the odds to make something out of nothing – in spite of a daily struggle to meet the world's demands. You are the unsung heroes and heroines who are destined to rise above all trial and tribulations.

USER'S GUIDE

How to use the quotations in the passage

1. Bible & General Quotations

"There are different kinds of gifts, but the same Spirit distributes them. There are different kinds of services, but we serve the same Lord. There are different kinds of working, but in all of them and in everyone it is the same God at work,"1 Corinthians 12: 4 –6.

2. Author (Moses Moreroa)'s Quotations

Before you were born, God has set you aside. God has made you uniquely different. God gave you the power to make the best out of your life. Start to stop saying you are not. Defeat your fears and try something new today.

Start to stop saying you are not.

Take responsibility and say you are who you think you are. You are a winner. You are better in the future. You are something that is beyond comparison.

Fingerprints develop at the time of conception. And fingerprints are matchless, even those of identical twins. So, you are what your fingerprint says you are – different and irreplaceable. You were born exclusive.

How to use the questions in the margin for every passage in every unit.

1. OPEN

This is intended to get you ready and to build your expectations of the chapter. Try to answer the questions honestly before starting to read. More than a starter, this part raises questions of concern. The questions are supposed to be answered according to your personal experiences, observations, perspective and, most importantly, through your profound judgement of situations.

2. DIGEST

After attempting to answer the OPEN questions, DIGEST makes you think, your current situation, a bit deeper to understand how you see things – and wish for them to turn out a certain way. It gives you the opportunity to think about the things you want as you prepare for the future. . You start separating the good from the bad.

3. RELATE helps you to remember a certain occasion in your life that relates to the unit you are reading. Recalling a certain event in your life, or relating this text to your own story, makes you engage your feelings and thoughts to encourage to think about the way you handled the situation in question, as well as, helping you to contemplate how you would handle it again should it happen.

And we know that in all things God works for the good of those who love him, who have been called according to his purpose – Romans 8:28

1

OPEN

1. Are you excellent in what you do?
2. Are you happy with your work, be it school, working place or artistically?
3. Have you ever received an excellence award?

2

DIGEST

1. What do you think constitutes excellence?
2. Mention any two advantages and disadvantages of excellence.
3. If you were to reward excellence, what would you first look at, in any situation of your choice?

3

RELATE

1. Have you ever felt like you have been excellent at your work but not recognised? What happened?
2. When last did you see

At one team building session, I requested a one-on-one session with the employees to find out about their habits. I wanted to know about their organisational culture, not that on policy but in person. I did the same with a few more companies. I have realised that in many organisations, employees get to work late. You get to work at 08h00 and start by making coffee. One company even had a tea society. At around 9h30 they get done with coffee and start making a few personal calls. Typically, each employee started working at around 10h00. And went for an official tea break at 11h00, typically working half a day every day.

And I told them that God rewards excellence. Their behaviour was standing against their promotion. But being excellent does not mean you are perfect. It means you pay attention to detail and do the right thing.

Being excellent simply means one improves by the day. Some people wonder why they don't get promotion, not knowing that their line managers were watching.

Thomas Edison tried two thousand different materials in search of a filament for the light bulb. When none worked satisfactorily, his assistant complained, "All our work is in vain. We have learned nothing." Edison replied very confidently, "Oh, we have come a long way and we have learned a lot. We know that there are two thousand elements which we cannot use to make a good light bulb." Now that element number two thousand and one was the right one, God blessed it so it can live longer and benefit the generations to come.

If you are at the same level, you don't improve at your work, you

I've learned . . .

By Omer B. Washington

In LIFE I've learned – that you cannot make someone love you. All you can do is be someone who can be loved. The rest is up to them. I've learned – that no matter how much I care, some people just don't care back.

I've learned – that it takes years to build up trust, and only seconds to destroy it. I've learned – that no matter how good a friend is, they're going to hurt you every once in a while and you must forgive them for that.

I've learned – that it's not what you have in your life but who you have in your life that counts. I've learned – that you should never ruin an apology with an excuse.

I've learned – that you can get by on charm for about fifteen minutes. After that, you'd better know something. I've learned – that you shouldn't compare yourself to the best others can do.

I've learned – that you can do something in an instant that will give you heartache for life. I've learned – that it's taking me a long time to become the person I want to be.

I've learned – that you should always leave loved ones with loving words. It may be the last time you see them. I've learned – that I've learned that you can keep going long after you can't. I've learned – that we are responsible for what we do, no matter how we feel. I've learned – that I've learned - that either you control your attitude or it controls you.

I've learned – that I've learned - that regardless of how hot and steamy a relationship is at first, the passion fades and there had better be something else to take its place.

I've learned – that heroes are the people who do what has to be done when it needs to be done, regardless of the consequences. I've learned – that money is a lousy way of keeping score. I've learned – that my best friend and I can do anything or nothing and have the best time. I've learned – that sometimes the people you expect to kick you when you're down will be the ones to help you get back up.

I've learned – that sometimes when I'm angry I have the right to be angry, but that doesn't give me the right to be cruel. I've learned – that true friendship continues to grow, even over the longest distance. Same goes for true love.

I've learned – that just because someone doesn't love you the way you want them to, doesn't mean they don't love you with all they have. I've learned – that maturity has more to do with what types of experiences you've had and what you've learned from them and less to do with how many birthdays you've celebrated.

I've learned – that you should never tell a child their dreams are unlikely or outlandish. Few things are more humiliating, and what a tragedy it would be if they believed it. I've learned – that your family won't always be there for you. It may seem funny, but people you aren't related to can take care of you and love you and teach you to trust people again. Families aren't biological.

I've learned – that it isn't always enough to be forgiven by others. Sometimes you must learn to forgive yourself. I've learned - that no matter how bad your heart is broken the world doesn't stop for your grief.

I've learned - that our background and circumstances may have influenced who we are, but we are responsible for who we become. I've learned - that a rich person is not the one who has the most, but is one who needs the least.

I've learned - that just because two people argue, it doesn't mean they don't love each other. And just because they don't argue, it doesn't mean they do. I've learned - that we don't have to change friends if we understand that friends change.

I've learned - that you shouldn't be so eager to find out a secret. It could change your life forever. I've learned - that two people can look at the exact same thing and see something totally different.

I've learned - that no matter how you try to protect your children, they will eventually get hurt and you will hurt in the process. I've learned - that even when you think you have no more to give, when a friend cries out to you, you will find the strength to help.

I've learned - that credentials on the wall do not make you a decent human being. I've learned - that the people you care about most in life are taken from you too soon. I've learned - that it's hard to determine where to draw the line between being nice and not hurting people's feelings, and standing up for what you believe.

I've learned - that people will forget what you said, and people will forget what you did, but people will never forget how you made them feel.

LEARN

Contents

ACKNOWLEDGEMENTS

To Jesus Christ, who is my success. Through his unfailing love I got wisdom that enabled me to write this book.

Rebecca Putla Nogane Mokibelo, I got all the courage from you. When you thought I was not looking, I saw your courage, commitment and hard work, and I decided to emulate it. I could not have asked for a better single mother. This goes to you and your late husband who went to live with the Lord when I was learning to speak the word "father". You have since played both the mother and father figure. *Ke a leboga mme motswadi, makoko!*

To my priest Abel Moreroa, whom I normally call Father, but is my biological brother.

And the rest of the family, Kgwashipe, Mathoga, Makeagane, and Kgaogelo. Special thanks for your teachings, guidance – and most importantly, your prayers.

To the House of the Twelve Apostles Church of Africa, which provided me with priceless wisdom and teachings of serving God's noble purpose.

My nieces and nephews – Dikeledi, Dineo, Khomotso, Thabang, Tokollo, Kimollo, Mamare, Florah, Nthabi, Junior and Primrose – your honesty when I used to ask you questions and your existence made me study the development of a human being and afforded me the opportunity to construct some growth models using my experiences with you.

Finally, to the people who transformed their calamities into fortune, this is to say *"I see you"*. Keep on keeping on. Your stories, some of which I shared in this book, have been my pillar of strength. *Le bogale*, as Isaac Ceeloo Mashila often says.

FOREWORD BY THEMBINKOSI PANTSI
Executive and Dealer Principal: Audi Centre Polokwane

PERSONAL NOTE

Firstly, let me congratulate you my dear friend and brother, Moses Moreroa, for the wonderful work you have done with this prosperity guide - Success Comes in Seven Pieces.

I felt honoured and privileged when you asked me to write the foreword to this magnificent piece.

Moses, you have precisely demonstrated the true meaning of living a life with "purpose". In this day and age, people get caught up between life with a purpose and not knowing their purpose. This book reflects nothing but a life with a purpose and I thank God that I have met you. Being one of the first people to read your book is amazing.

And this for me is a treasure I am adding to my collection of good reads.

Indeed, Glory is to God for ushering you into the earth realm for His name to be praised and glorified.

TO THE READER

This is not just an ordinary book. An everyday inspiration guide that is well placed to shape the life of the reader, forever. The practicality herein reflects how the author used his lived experiences, and the impact he wanted to make to the world, to come up with the book of this magnitude.

The central message is how one needs to manage all aspects of his or her life.

The book acknowledges that people hail from different backgrounds. Hence, it was in a way that allows everyone to locate the depths of their conditions and emerge prosperously. Like as in the 'Wheel of Life Approach', this book entails action steps that help the reader to have goals and invent models or ways in which the pursuit of success becomes inevitable.

As you read on from one chapter to another, you will realise that Moses has indeed produced a guideline that involves the steps one needs to take as they climb their own 'Kilimanjaro Mountain.' As the climbers of Kilimanjaro would say, "Pole-Pole", step by step, slowly but surely you will get there.

For me, this is what humankind needs to possess in order to develop a character of doing rather than expecting an overnight success. Success comes after one shall have sweated hard enough.

This book implores everyone who dares to dream that success is not for the selected few, as some tend to believe. All of us are wired and destined to be successful.

This stellar work reminds me that with good plans in place, hard work, good character, dedication, focus, and perseverance, everything is possible. We can all be successful.

No matter where you come from, no matter how your background is or was, success is possible and "SUCCESS COMES IN SEVEN PIECES". Find the right piece at a time and build your castle.

I truly believe and trust that you will be inspired as I am by the work that Moses Moreroa has produced, which is one of the best books I have ever read.

ENJOY!

MESSAGE OF SUPPORT FROM MATODZI MAKANANISA
CEO at Limpopo Media House and F.A.M.E Awards

The first time I encountered the author of this book, Moses Moreroa, was through Facebook in 2014. Moreroa had commented on my post about a homeless man who was reading a piece about success.

Brian Nkuzana, who later became my mentee, had been homeless for a week when I met him in the streets of Polokwane, where a group of young homeless men created for themselves a "makeshift home".

So determined to turn his challenges upside down, Brian had undergone several interviews for a graphic designer post and hoped to get a response before going back home in Giyani.

This book reminded me of Brain. He refused to be miserable amid life challenges. He was homeless but did not beg for food or money. He read and sharpened his mind even in the most uncomfortable surroundings. What was important for him was to prepare for a future of possibilities.

This is what I found in Chapter 1 where the author asked if whether the glass is half-full or half-empty. The chapter beseeches the reader to understand the stage of life he or she is in. Brian understood the stage he was in and knew that nothing in life was permanent. Hence, today he is running a thriving business in Thohoyandou.

In 2002, I dropped out of the University of Limpopo owing to financial difficulties. When I got home, my father sat me down and apologised for failing to plan for my future. I looked at him with sadness straddling my face and apologised, too.

I apologised for not trying harder. I apologised for going home to sleep when I could have been out there exploring ways to turn my situation around.

Chapter 2 is called "I AM". Now that you shall have figured out your situation, the chapter says it is time to take charge, no matter the situation. I found myself relating closely to the content because I refused to fall into the trap of self-pity. I refused to ride on my father's apology.

Whether you are sent to school or not, it is still up to you to work hard. Everyone today is a product of their circumstances and decisions, not a product of the conditions in which they were born into.

I want you to pay attention to a section where Moses talks about driving own ship, which comprises relationship, entrepreneurship, dictatorship, mentorship, and friendship. For you to succeed in life, you need to be in a good space.

Keep your circle positive. In order to get ahead in life, let go of old negative habits, including people that no longer add value to your life. Make space for new "useful" people in your life, like a mentor.

Success is also a result of well-calculated risks. If you are not willing to take a risk, then you are not ready for success. Moses says risk is everywhere and anywhere. To live, be to risk death, to walk is to risk falling. So, why not continue because everything is risky?

In my life, I have made several of grave mistakes. I once sold majority shares to a group of white men from Gauteng. They later frustrated me and when I challenged their decisions, charges were built-up against me.

I was eventually fired from my own company. This taught me that success is pursuing one thing after the next, without a loss of enthusiasm and grit.

Finally yet importantly, be disciplined. Many of us from the so-called previously disadvantaged groups are our own worst enemies. When I saw my first million, I found myself buying things I did not need. By the time, I thought of investment, I had wasted a quarter of that figure.

This is why Moses dedicated a full chapter to mentorship. He guides as to how one can pick a mentor, how to sustain relations in a mentorship and when to be independent. Mentorship Is not only physical but also spiritual.

The best new "best friend" in your success is not a drinking friend. Moses in the last chapter says God is your success. Get closer to God. Let Him lead your ways and see your territory enlarge.

A PERSONAL LETTER TO READERS

Dear Ambitious Friend,

What struggles do you face today? Pain? Worry? Financial oppression? Lack of confidence, courage, commitment or faith? Do you have fear, of something known or unknown? Are you expecting a miracle in your life?

I came to the realisation that the majority of the people have neglected their responsibilities and shifted answerability to God. God never performs miracles in our lives.

He gives us power to perform miracles. We should pray for strength rather than miracles.

Also, enough about humble beginnings. Almost all of us come from destitute backgrounds. The glorious stories about rags to riches or zero to hero do not help us become better people: they inspire us.

These stories can only provide us with encouragement, gladness and hope, but cannot change us completely if we do not realise that our future is self-determined.

That said, action, rather than motivation as the popular belief alleges, is the most effective tool to create a better future as we work to set our life on a fine trajectory.

We are better off without lip service cheerleaders. We need mentors who can teach people how to do things rather than informing them how others did things. That is the reason Thembinkosi Pantsi was best positioned to write the foreword to this book – he has proven on numerous occasions to be such a visionary who triggers action through leadership.

Pantsi believes in action and understands that life becomes more meaningful when we do not only seek inspiration but work towards testing our solutions and formulas to life.

Today, he is the Executive and Principal Dealer at the newly opened Audi Centre Polokwane. He even uses his facility to empower small business owners who do not have official offices to conduct meetings and other business-related activities.

Use this book as an ingredient to a successful life, your transformation gear. It will teach you how life develops and make you trace your moves from the beginning.

This book is informed by how today's generation who appear wealthy, intelligent, goal-oriented, and in control from the outside but are consumed by fear, uncertainty, revenge, envy, jealousy, excuses, dissatisfaction, and discomfort on the inside.

From the beginning, we discover that all things are possible. Let us cherish the idea that all men were created in the image of God, which makes talent a birthright.

In essence, everyone has a gift from God that is meant to help him or her succeed in life. We are meant to succeed.

I have realised that people tend to hide behind the words; *God will make a way*, when they want to avoid working.

I wish you could partner with God in your journey to success. When one hopes for a better future in His name, He is with them. You are good enough to achieve all your dreams.

After all, God does not call the qualified, but He qualifies the called. When you partner with Him, He will qualify you in every aspect of your life, including the areas of education, career, relationships, and marriage.

The only thing you must know is that success is like a puzzle, and you need to figure it out one step at a time. But start by seeing the bigger picture.

Many people move around instead of moving on because they have not found their purpose. Purpose is like gold. It is not found anywhere.

Finding your purpose comes through having an intimate relationship with God and having a better understanding of yourself as a human being.

As I have noted earlier, other people spend most of their time moving around – aimlessly conducting their orchestra without the presence of the Father - rather facing their realities and seeking to understand their identities in Christ.

Before we can think about finding our purpose, we need to understand the reason behind creation and how this is connected to our existence.

There must be an idea where purpose could be, followed by digging. My prayer for you is this. That through these trying times – amid many pressures, be they economic, social, or psychological – may you find strength, courage and hope to fulfil your life purpose.

INTRODUCTION

The book is organised in seven user-friendly chapters, which Moses christened "pieces of success". Through them, one learns how unsuccessful people got it wrong, and how successful people stood out in their pursuit of God, business, and wealth.

There is just one route or procedure that successful people follow. Believe you me, to be unsuccessful you have to go through a lot!

There are ten steps that unsuccessful people go through in order to make sure that they fail in life. They firstly learn to doubt, commit mistakes, and then sink into regrets, discontent, disappointments, idleness, hatred, pain, lack, and dishonesty until there is a glimmer of hope for the future.

These ten steps are summarised in five stages in the first chapter – play and imitation, education and self-discovery, dedication and adventure, drive your own ship, and wisdom and wealth.

Before starting on the stages, it will be advisable to analyse your current situation.

This inspirational guide offers practical principles of putting together a winning recipe. It takes you through all stages of life from birth to infancy, adolescence, adulthood, career choices, moulding your career and retirement.

It is your successful guide summarised in seven effective pieces. Very practical in nature, the book offers various models you can apply to achieve your dreams, of course, with the help of God.

The chapters, referred to as pieces, are linked from the first to the last. Yours is to read and discover the stage of your life and therefore take it from there going to the last chapter which is probably your last days of life.

For easy navigation, when you OPEN the first page of each chapter, start using key pointers on the chapter page. After you have guessed the content of the chapter, sit back, read and reflect on your life.

Make a to-do annual plan and set goals for yourself. Use the book to get ideas on how and where to start with your dream. Set timelines to your plan so you can gauge if there is progress or if you have been sluggish.

The guide contains well-thought-out life lessons where every chapter will require you to relate with your own story.

Each chapter will teach you the basics of learning to make something great out of your situation.

It will help you to deal with your slow growth, negativity from others and, most importantly, negativity within you.

It will also teach you to confront your fears while reshaping your lifestyle, managing your relationships and discovering your life deeply.

In the first piece, there is a section where you are taught how to steer your "ship", which has five components – relationship or companionship, friendship, mentorship, entrepreneurship, and dictatorship.

EARLY BIRDS

Lucid. Practical. Specific. Moses uses his experience as a life coach, professional communicator and spiritual leader to tell us about the way we formulate meanings and generate perspectives that create opportunities and failures for our life.

Life, as he captures it through stages and pieces, can be changed for the better through this practical guide, as people will learn to question their own perspective to life.

His story resonates with the story of a man who died of thirst on the bank of a healthy river because it did not occur to him that the river carried water.

This book is praiseworthy from different angles: Moses uses fresh yet effective language to drive his ideas home and cut through life and its sharp vicissitude from different angles, covering culture, business, psychology, and education.

Metji Makgoba -
Commonwealth Scholar at Cardiff University, Wales, UK.

Endorsements

Whether you have finer things in life or not, this book is a great motivator, mentor, and worth keeping. It is packaged in a way that one is propelled to pause and reflect on their life, then continue to read about various success models that Moses has developed.

It makes the reader interrogate his or her progress in life. Of course, Moses believes all is possible with God. This is a must read.

Athanatious "Mr Flamboyant" Masoma –
Media Personality

Success Comes In Seven Pieces is one of the first books to guide people, irrespective of age, through a dark, twisted and hilarious journey called life. Not only does the tone of the book match a leader oozing confidence, it cuddles the same satirical sense of humour. I should say Moses has written a must-read primer, more like a therapy for all human lacks.

Zaxe Mogashoa -
Meener Kgokong on Mahlakung Soapie & Moshe on
Takalani Sesame – Thobela FM

Endorsements

It is so rare to find a book that directly speaks to your life. This book outstandingly mastered this art. Reading the book forces you to do some self-introspection to assess your growth in life. And since God is competent, Moses endorses The Almighty as the only shuttle that can usher one from any negative situation to glory. No winner without a coach. Moses explains this need and guides the reader towards choosing the right mentor. If you are looking to reach greater heights in your life, then look no further than this book.

Makeagane Moreroa –

Sister

This book is impeccable for any person trying to negotiate his or her way to success. It makes you understand that life throws two kinds of pressures at you – negative and positive. Pressure can burst a pipe and equally produce a diamond. The book teaches you to make the best out of your situation.

Kgaogelo "Kay" Sebola –

CEO at Reconnect Day Spa

Endorsements

Firstly, I have to say I could not get my eyes off the book. It perfectly guides you into what you are looking for. It's a good read. How do we define success? The seven chapters in this book take you on a journey from birth to death. I have to agree with the author on most aspects raised in this book and pour out some of my own thoughts. We all have 24 hours, so what makes us different? There are dreams and dream-sellers, so be careful of the person next to you. I believe this book will take you through all the steps of life as it is not only well written but perfectly narrated. Allow to me lacuna and have my Three Ships: Friendship, Relationship, and Entrepreneurship.

Sontaga Letshelele –
Media Personality

What excites me the most is the way Moses balanced the act of life. If you feel like your dreams are unlikely to happen, the book explains how you got it wrong and what to do to succeed. His theories of success are certainly a reality. This splendid work does an incredible job of creating a sense of urgency in the reader. A must read indeed.

Pam Ditshego –
Media Personality

Say no to a "microwave success". This book reminds me of my journey in the radio industry. I have discovered that real success is a process and cannot be attained instantly. In the case of radio, the producer works on a script, which is development.

The script is then sent to the chief producer for fine-tuning. The programmes manager approves what the chief has polished. And the presenter has to be LIT.

This is what this book is all about. It teaches you to first identify your situation, gather resources, get mentorship and sharpen your thoughts, and develop your craft. You have to put together all of these pieces to have a great success.

Isaac Ceeloo Mashila –
Radio Personality

First Piece

IS THE GLASS HALF FULL OR HALF EMPTY?

First Piece: Is The Glass Half Full Or Half Empty?

Christopher McCandless: So many people live within unhappy circumstances and yet will not take the initiative to change their situation because they are conditioned to a life of security, conformity, and conservation, all of which may appear to give one peace of mind, but in reality, nothing is more damaging to the adventurous spirit.

Matthew 15:11: That which goes into someone's mouth does not defile them, but what comes out of their mouth, that is what defiles them.

First Piece: Is The Glass Half Full Or Half Empty?

Every situation is useless, senseless, worthless, hopeless and pointless until you give it a meaning with significance and purpose so you can make impact. In life, there is an interpretation to every situation. How you construe and draw conclusions about things in your environs is how you will eventually live up to your views and expectations.

For instance, if you were to send two journalists to report on a protest by Mankweng residents at Unit G, who have barricaded a road. How the two will describe the event is entirely dependent on their frame of mind.

One reporter could say, "It's chaotic. The situation is tense. Roads are blocked. People are desperate. The situation is only going to get worse." But the other might report: "The SAPS and the municipal manager are trying to reach out to the protesters. They are urging them to voice their grievances in a civilised manner, so that the matter can be resolved."

One day, an English professor wrote the words: "A woman without her man is nothing" on the chalkboard and asked the students to punctuate it correctly.

All of the males in the class wrote: "A woman, without her man, is nothing."

All of the females in the class wrote: "A woman: without her, man is nothing."

From these experiences, you would realise that, in every situation, one takes a certain point of view, relying mostly on their frame of mind, past experiences and future intentions. These frames are also known as mental models of a cultural mind that dictates how people attach meaning - or the lack thereof – to different social events.

To determine if a figure is a 6 or 9, one has to take a particular stance. In the extreme, Tim Burton, the ninth-highest-grossing director by worldwide box office, states that "One person's craziness is another person's reality."

In my village, Segwashi, Ga-Mamabolo, across a nursery farm that is owned by Van der Merwe, there is a bridge that gets muddy when it rains, especially overnight. Motorists in the early hours of the morning usually compete with each other to be the first to pass through the muddy road because the road becomes a quagmire once the first car churns up the soft surface.

Unfortunately, one day as I was driving to work, I found, to my bewilderment, that other people have churned up the mud with their cars. I did not have other options but to scrape through the mud, I drove in.

I put the car on the first gear hoping that it would negotiate the way quite smoothly but the opposite happened. My car began to bog down spreading particles of wet soils and dirty water around and making an unusual sound as if I was climbing a hill. And the more I accelerated, the rear wheels just spun and dug deeper into the mud. The rain started pouring again. I was stuck. And I was going to be late for work. Then, a white man, clad in khaki shorts exemplifying an image of a local farmer, arrived from the opposite direction driving a Land Cruiser.

He offered to tow me out of the jam for R300. My suit was very slim after BroTailor had resized it, and I could not risk getting it dirty. I knew that R360 was exactly my last money for the month, but I agreed to pay the price. He helped me out.

As I went on to the tarred road, two people asked for a lift to Turfloop. I stopped and they quickly hopped into the car. As we drove to our destination, one cautioned me for speeding. I told them how the mud and rain had delayed me and that I was late for work.

After listening to my explanation, the person who did not complain about my speed, commented, "At least, rain is a blessing from God. My mother always prayed for the rain when the mealies were dying in the heat."

As I was about to respond, the one who complained about my speeding, added that it should only rain at night because God knows we all have to go to work and do other things for a living.

As we passed Zion City Moria, we saw a Bahwaduba Bus that was going to Segwashi at Viking.

The two started talking about how the bus will obviously return without a single person because no one would brave such rain.

The bus usually makes a U-turn at the tarred road when it's raining and does not go inside the village because the road is badly maintained. People are forced to walk about five kilometres to the tarred road.

As we continued with the journey, at Mentz, there was someone fixing his shack and putting bricks on the roof. His actions suggested that there was a strong wind in the area. People put bricks on their roofs to compensate for bad workmanship, ensuring that the roof does not fly with the blowing gale.

When I got to work, I did not even tell anyone about my terrible morning.

The moral lesson behind this true story is that everyone has a particular view of life depending on their frame of mind and circumstances. There were other complex problems, bigger than mine, which people experienced because of rain and perhaps the gale.

For some, the rain was wonderful because their produce would be nourished and grow. But it also left other people with mixed emotions or an air of ambivalence as you have seen in my small talk with the people who drove with me to Turfloop.

One of them said that although the rain was wonderful for their mother's crops, it was not good for their health, complaining about pneumonia-related problems.

First Piece: Is The Glass Half Full Or Half Empty?

The farmer, who got me out of the quagmire, saw the rain as an opportunity to make quick cash. On the other hand, the Bahwaduba Bus owner experienced financial losses: it used fuel to go to the village but only to return with few commuters to make a profit.

A man at Mentz had to go out in the rain to fix his shack. To the people who had reservoirs and tanks to store water, the rain brought pleasure.

These thoughts made me realise that our situations will never be the same, even under similar circumstances. The same rain caused joy, confusion, blessings or trouble for different people, depending on what it did to them.

Just like nature and its mysteries, our life presents us with challenges and opportunities that condition our mind, attitude and behaviour to have a certain cultural and social arrangement.

For instance, if we were to ask people from different occupations whether a half glass of water was half-full or half-empty, the responses are going to be critically different and telling.

Instead of giving you an answer, a receptionist is likely to ask if you do not mind waiting while they are going to find out for you from their superiors. This is because, in most cases, receptionists are never given the opportunity to take decisions: they tend to refer matters to the next person who is responsible.

A politician is likely to say, "I found the glass getting even emptier. Now that I am around, it is half-full. I just need more time around it for it to be full." It is in their nature; politicians firstly discredit the next person to secure their standpoint and support in life.

An actor, because of their artistic ambitions, albeit highly managed, may say that "however, and whatever, the owner wants it to be, it is fine either way." Actors never take charge of their act. Their action is the result of someone who thinks on their behalf, the director. They always listen to instruction and act. So, whatever the director says goes.

An engineer might say the size of the glass might be too big for the required amount of water. The first thing would be to examine the glass and the water and take measurements. To them the water should have been out of the glass to allow the gauging of the quantity and ultimately design a glass that would match the amount of the water. They believe in accuracy.

A magician sees the glass as half-full from the top going down, simply because where everybody else sees none, magicians turn things around, or upside down, and perform the unexpected. They enjoy doing the opposite and mostly the unthinkable.

On the other hand, a waiter takes the glass, empties it and cleans for the next customer to use. It doesn't matter to them if it's half full or half empty, their task is to clean up the table. What matters is: when the glass left the kitchen, it went as a full order because the bill says so.

Learners see the glass as another trick played by the teacher to prove that every learner is dumb until the teacher opens their eyes.

First Piece: Is The Glass Half Full Or Half Empty?

Learners always think teachers ask useless questions even when they have answers. Which seems a waste of time to them.

A fool or nyaope addict does not care. He says as long as there is something in the glass they will take it and do anything to it. Even if it's laughing at the glass.

Someone who depends on another is concerned about who is going to fill the glass if it's half empty. And who is filling it, if it's filling up. They never want to be part of the action but enjoy seeing the results.

I could go on and on about every profession or kind of people. And I wouldn't finish until the end of the world. Just imagine what a police man would say, not to mention a doctor or a hairdresser.

Obviously, a pastor will say that God will provide. The glass will be full because it is a year of increase, double glory. A year of multiplication. A year of harvest. God will see it through. This is because men of God believe God is the provider of everything.

Truth is, the glass is neither half full nor half empty. It depends on the meaning each person gives it. The problem, or the solution, depends on how you see a particular situation.

In every situation, there is that one person who thinks he or she is progressive yet they are far behind the times. They never learn, and complain about any challenge. There is also that one person who, however, learns from every situation and improves.

Every situation brings with it success and failure. It only depends on who is in that situation and what they say about it. How you see your situation and what you do about it is entirely up to you. There are people who start off as brilliant - on the right path, but when they get to a situation where they have to change the path, they become reluctant and static.

If you were to tie up a cat and put it on the road, cars would run it over. Same goes for a person who is on the right track but doesn't progress. If you have remained in the same position or stage, whether right or wrong, you are prone to feelings of frustration, discouragement and exasperation – which will drive you nuts and prepare you for destruction

Understand your situation. When you complain about your situation, someone somewhere is embracing it – and happy about being in the same situation. Never measure your dreams against that of the person next.

"There are different kinds of gifts, but the same Spirit distributes them. There are different kinds of services, but we serve the same Lord. There are different kinds of working, but in all of them and in everyone it is the same God at work,"1 Corinthians 12: 4 -6.

Priest AS Moreroa of The House of the Twelve Apostles quoted this in a sermon. It was delivered on Mothers' Day. He said people develop jealousy, hatred and anxiety because they do not know their purpose in life.

It is because we are yet to discover that we cannot have people's gifts unless God gave us. Put differently, other people cannot have the same gifts as ours. Life is not designed that way.

Finding on the people's gifts is destructive and usually encourages people to develop inferiority complex and negative emotions. It also diverts us from discovering and developing our own gifts, as well as, causing us to forgot about why we were created in the first place. After all, our gifts are meant to supplement one another to make the world a better place.

For other people, this teaches them to focus on what they do not have, causing to forget what God has already provided. Hence, we have people who pay money for other people to speak to God on their behalf.

It does not occur to them that they can simply kneel down and pray.

Priest Moreroa said gifts are discovered at work. Like a teacher who wants to know the understanding of their learners, they teach and then ask oral questions to confirm whether they understand what has been taught.

When learners give adequate answers, the teacher would consider setting a test. This is to assess if the learners can explain through writing.

This is to say we only realise our capabilities through acting upon our ideas in different ways. Someone may be able to describe something in speech but may fail to do the same in writing. That's being unable to thrive from one situation to the next.

To understand your situation is to learn all about both your weaknesses and strengths. Build on your strong links and seek help to overthrow your weaknesses.

Do not get so familiar with your weakness, or negative situation, to the extent that you do not see it as a problem anymore.

Accepting your bad situation and problem as common and familiar reduces your potential of building a good future.

The decision you make about your current situation determines your future. Think about it.

You were not born in an impossible situation. It is the ideas you listened to along the way that make you lack courage, and the ability to make progress in your life.

Life is a cycle: you need to keep on moving from one stage to another. Developing an understanding of the different stages of life can help you better explain your current situation and the challenges it presents.

It is important to understand that your situation, even though it feels and looks *ayoba*, can act as a trap that prevents you from developing.

In the same breath, the situation you find yourself in now can be the next step to greater heights. It all depends on what you decide to do and act on the decision.

It is highly possible for an old person to be trapped in the first stage of life whereas a young person can double his or her steps forward.

First Piece: Is The Glass Half Full Or Half Empty?

Use the following model, which comprises five key stages of life, to become aware of the situation you are in.

First Piece: Is The Glass Half Full Or Half Empty?

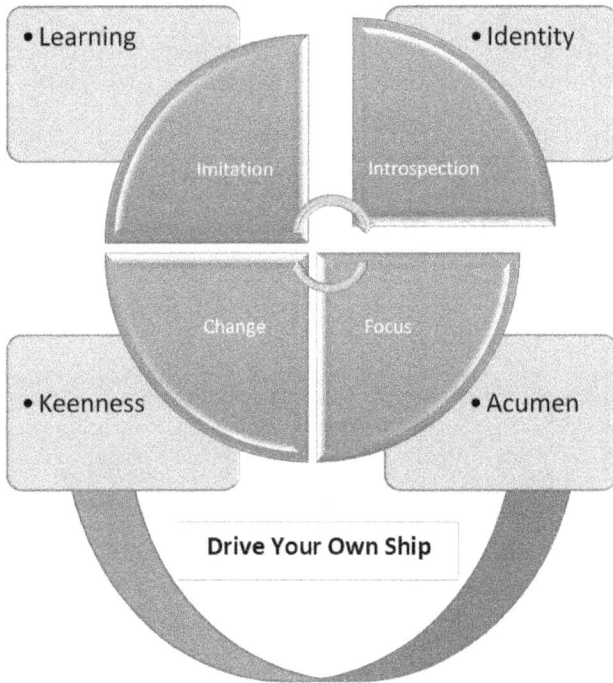

- Learning
- Identity

Imitation

Introspection

Change

Focus

- Keenness
- Acumen

Drive Your Own Ship

Mosian Progression Phases

The above model represents five phases of life, namely Learning (imitation and fear), Identity (self-awareness and crisis), Keenness (change and goal-orientation), Acumen (focus and perfectionism), and Drive Your Own Ship (maturity and independence).

*Dubbed **Mosian Model** – a combination of three words: **Mo**reroa **Si**tuation **An**alysis – the model in and of itself is a life journey not even a single person can avoid. It is important to note that some get stuck in one stage for too long whereas others skip some stages. But in any case, one gets to go through the stages nonetheless, sooner or later. No wonder you have seen a child somewhere behaving like an adult and vice versa.*

First Piece: Is The Glass Half Full Or Half Empty?

Negativity brews fear and getting drunk
on fear is not the best feeling ever.

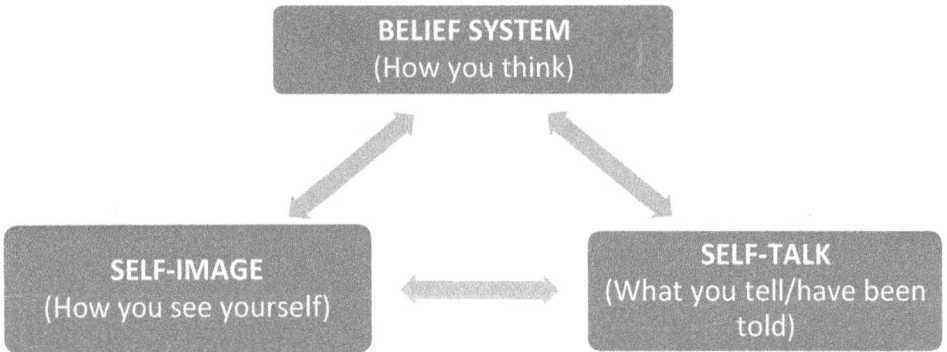

BELIEF SYSTEM
(How you think)

SELF-IMAGE
(How you see yourself)

SELF-TALK
(What you tell/have been told)

OPEN

1. What do you think constitutes knowledge?
2. If you were given powers to regulate what knowledge is, how would you facilitate the process?
3. Between formal education and informal learning, which one do you prefer and why?

DIGEST

1. When first did you feel so proud that you gained knowledge? What did you gain?

RELATE

1. When last did you feel like learning was not important? Why?
2. When last did you imitate someone?

I remember a teaching by District Letsoalo of the Twelve Apostles on 16 April 2017. He said life starts with knowledge. No one is either wrong or right until they know the difference between good or bad.

This is exactly what the first stage of life is all about – learning takes place by doing, and often the imitation process results in knowledge.

This stage focuses on the beginning – birth, infancy, childhood and early education. It is all about learning. Like a baby, we observe other people's behaviour and imitate their actions. This helps us to pick up important abilities and skills. By impersonating or copycatting, we gradually develop social and similar skills and learn to fit in society.

As toddlers, rules, thinking patterns and norms are imposed upon us and we are taught to behave, act, and often think in socially acceptable manners.

If you still start your talk by saying, "I am not sure if I am right... and I don't know how you will take this..." know that you are   too

16

apologetic about life and you don't hold authentic belief. Such people always think they are not good enough. Feeling not–good–enough reduces one's ability to act on their dreams. Such people often fear rejection or dismissal, which leads to lack of confidence.

Sometimes being dependent upon others for guidance and seeking their approval is as dangerous as sleeping wearing a tie. The greatest danger is that you struggle to find purpose in life. Because you think what you want to do is never good enough – if you don't do it the way you were taught and how others are doing it. The need for validation can be as dangerous as a Green Mamba; those who are unable to let go of it will certainly suffer.

If you relate to this narrative, know that you are trapped in the first stage of life. You have not developed and you definitely think like a child who has just started school and thinks she is nothing without the teacher.

Failing to outreach this stage makes you feel like an adolescent who needs to please others. You even post a picture of yourself on Facebook eating a pizza simply because you're trying to prove the point that you're your own man, but that comes across as childish.

Purpose is very personal. If, at this moment, you still value other people's opinions above your own, you have a great burden upon your shoulders. Because you will always feel obliged to conform. And the result is that you will never have the courage to embark on your journey.

There is no inner peace without purpose.

Break free from this burden in the first stage of life by refusing to let someone else define your destiny and dictate your thoughts. Passion and purpose are often uncovered by doing things your own way. You get to learn about what you can – and cannot do.

When you leave high school, you must have finished doing everything foolish. If you go on to tertiary and drink alcohol until you lose your room key . . . Sorry – but there's a child trapped in that huge body of yours. To be precise, at the age of 17, you should be waving goodbye to this stage.

WHAT HAPPENS IN THIS STAGE	WHY YOU GET STUCK	HOW TO MOVE ON
Trying to fit in	Need approval from others	Appreciate your uniqueness
Belief in others/role models	Lack of creativity	Try new things, your way
Feeling not good enough	Fear of the unknown	Develop genuine qualities
Do things to please others	Lack of priority	Think independently

Stage 2: Identity

OPEN

1. What is Identity?
2. How would you describe yourself in one sentence?

DIGEST

1. Have you ever thought as if you were living two lives?
2. If you were to change one thing about yourself, what would it be?

RELATE

1. How did you see yourself when you were in Grade 12? Are you the same person today?

It is not very bad to be in the previous stage where you solely depend on education and try to imitate those you call role models or hold high in your dreams.

It only turns out to be bad when you prolong your stay in that stage. The stage is not meant to cage you but to help you quickly develop your own ideas and images of the future.

The second stage is all about experimentation. It is now the right place to try new things and despise other things. At this stage, like an adolescent or teenager, you act against the expectations of others.

You start being too serious about life but you are not sure about the life you think you are serious about. Often people in this stage start thinking about family, career, and favourite cars and so on.

What is important about this stage is that it is mostly confusing. I know someone wonders what would be great in confusion.

Imagine you're in a new place and not sure about where you're supposed to go. You start looking around, pretending you're sure of

19

yourself. You are afraid to ask around because you either fear exposing your vulnerability to things like being mugged, or taken for a fool. You end up reading signposts, names of buildings and counting the streetlights.

At the same time, you make sure your belongings are protected. You are ready to run for safety should anything suspicious happen. In short, you are vigilant.

This stage often happens between the ages of 18 and 19. You know you are alone in the world and have to make decisions that will not only help the moment but also shape the future.

You go through what we call *identity crisis* and *role confusion*. You are looking to develop a sense of self and personal identity.

You start thinking about your future career, husband or wife, type of house and stuff like that. Life gets real. You can choose your study field by default, chance, and knowledge or otherwise, it doesn't matter. What matters is this: you want to make the most out of your choices.

WHAT HAPPENS IN THIS STAGE	WHY DO YOU GET STUCK	HOW TO MOVE ON
Sense of self-importance	Make bad decisions	Learn as you grow
Introspection	Pretending to be something	Identify mistakes
Role confusion, no clear life plan	Continue to pretend	Stick to one thing
Wish for finer things in life	Continue to pretend	Imagine your future

OPEN

1. Do you know what you want in life? Are you still trying to figure out what you can do best?

DIGEST

1. Do you have any regrets? Be it the study field you have chosen or things you should or shouldn't have done earlier?

RELATE

1. What was the last time you really thought you were behind in life? What was happening? Did you make peace with it? Do you still feel the same?

Stage 3: Keenness

This is a turning point for development. Here the prospect for growth is greater and so is the potential for failure. What you carry with you from the previous stage of self-discovery is important.

Some realise that they are not so good at something but remain stubborn and do not change. Some change for the better. How you take what you discovered is key at this stage.

The pursuit of your dreams has become more important to you than anything.

You will strive to make the most of your life by living up to your full potential.

You have in your attempt to be independent, gained experience, grew wiser and now understand the consequences of wasting time.

Now that you are about to go beyond teenage years, you have grown to understand the importance of saving money.

While, at this stage, you feel like you are sure of the things you want in your life, congratulations, you have made it to the next stage. It takes only a few months to get your life together.

Should you remain unsure of what you want, then you will always feel insecure and confused.

Insecurity and confusion lead to underdevelopment. Instead of developing, you going back to the first two stages where you just want to impersonate others and pretend to be on the right track.

Normally, you are in your early twenties at this stage; it is the longest phase in the human cycle.

You regret the things you did or did not do. Truth is, you are the outcome of two things – things you did and things you didn't do.

WHAT HAPPENS IN THIS STAGE	WHY DO YOU GET STUCK	HOW TO MOVE ON
Ambitious	Too confident	Research your goal
Regrets	Holding on to the past	Learn from past experiences
Making and meeting own decisions	Doubt	Stick to your decisions
Self appreciation	Fear of judgement	Dress to be addressed
Start to explore life	Wanting to be Jack of all trades	Take one step at a time
Education is completed	Lack of practicality	Practise what you learned

OPEN

1. What do you think sets you apart?
2. Are you at a level of independence or you still fear failure?

DIGEST

1. When last were you criticised? What happened? How did you take it?
2. What is one thing you really want to achieve in the next five years?

RELATE

1. What was your one time opportunity? Did it fall through or you made the best out of it?

Stage 4: Wisdom

Knowledge does not generate wealth. It is the use of knowledge that distinguishes us from the rest. The application of knowledge that helps us become strategic.

Being strategic means knowing when to use knowledge to your advantage, or for greater good. That is wisdom.

I equal wisdom to wealth. There is not even a single wise person who is poor. I do not mean the poor are foolish, but they simply did not use their knowledge to their advantage.

A diamond is nothing but a coal that did well under pressure. In your situation, you come out shining or too dark for people to see. How you apply your knowledge is critical at this stage.

A great shift in focus takes place. We place our concentration on that which is important to us while allowing the rest to leave our life.

Wisdom is not the absence of mistakes, but the ability to rise above an erroneous situation and continue with something else. A mistake can either be a correction or a lesson that you should not repeat what you have done.

People, at this stage, definitely know when to ignore the excitement as everything seems to be coming together. Good things often come in this stage, but mostly out of a true purpose.

When I started at the University of Limpopo I had all the wisdom I needed. Many more opportunities came, as most of the people could see the bright side in me.

It was exciting to be offered numerous opportunities. I started trying out new things, and lost the sight of my true purpose, which was to grow as a lecturer.

I started doing so many things at once and lost it all. I eventually got suspended by my line manager and arrogance led to my resignation before going to hearing. I since learned never to be a Jack of all trades while mastering none.

At this stage, you will make new discoveries. It is wisdom, only, that should help you calculate your moves. Not the arrogant attitude that you are the most diligent and trusted goal digger.

Pick what is significant about your future. Without noticing, you might run in circles. It does not help to be able to do many things – if there is no noticeable progress.

Wisdom comes with limitations. As you discover your talents, you will also discover the things you are not good at. We start to realise that many of the activities we have enjoyed for so long no longer provide us any significant returns.

We let go of the things that no longer meet our talents and ambitions.

At this stage, you make calculated moves and get rich. You misstep, you fall.

WHAT HAPPENS IN THIS STAGE	WHY DO YOU GET STUCK	HOW TO MOVE ON
Focus lies on the outside world	Fear of failure	Master one trade at a time
Accept responsibility	Choosing pleasure over goals	Only take what matters
Willingness to take risks	Taking uncalculated risks	Proper planning
Self-challenge	Failure to confront one's failures	Fail forward
Becoming independent and autonomous	Arrogance	Continuous learning
Criticism	Caring about people's opinion	Ignore resentment from others
Pride	Impressing needlessly	Be modest and get ahead

Stage 5: Drive Your Own Ship

OPEN

1. Are you in control of your life or you still want to be on good terms with others even when it compromises your priorities?
2. How would you describe your relationship, be it family, spiritual or sexual?

DIGEST

1. Why did you enter into the relationships you have currently?
2. Do you have a mentor? Is it useful or not?

RELATE

1. Ever gone against your boss, parents, and partner or church principles? When and what happened? Why?

A dream is like a ship. It solely wants to be kept afloat, moving to its destination. No matter how big or long the ship can be it has to rise above the pressure of sinking.

A ship has to jump higher than unpredictable waves. Its captain should not be perturbed by what is beneath the water because the ship's sole purpose is moving ahead.

Some boats depend on the wind to get a proper direction and balance. Some boats depend on the direction of waves to move forward.

Other boats need the sun to function. As the captain of your own ship, you need to, first, know the kind of boat you are steering and what it needs to get going.

The following five topics will help you understand your situation.

I hope you are going to make the right choices as you drive your ship.

Once you gain your independence and autonomy, you will often start to think that the world is at your mercy. You now have money and can afford most of the things. You start increasing responsibilities. You are in charge of your life, or so you think.

RELATIONSHIP/COMPANIONSHIP

There are countless kinds of relationships but I am more interested in the two which are most dangerous – biological and love. On one hand, your family might not believe in you, dispirit your drive, and dampen your hopes.

On the other hand, a codependent love affair can be draining.

At this stage, one's career is on the rise and the focus is no longer on making the best out of a career or one's talents. The focus becomes more on getting more money, finding a home and a partner.

The idea of settling down starts kicking in. The exploring, freedom and everything in stage three and four decrease dramatically as one looks to settle down.

A relationship with a girlfriend or a boyfriend can break or make you. Some have partners who are less ambitious. When you get paid and wish to save up for property, he or she wants a useless vacation.

He or she complains about you not making time for them because you too focused on your career. She or he is jealous when you mingle with potential business partners at a gala dinner.

Family can also disturb your progress. I know of a friend who hired most of his family in his new company at Honeydew in Gauteng. His relationship with them clouded his business ethics and professionalism.

The business collapsed because he could not put a stop to irregularities and unwillingness to put in any hard work.

Family members might also discourage you, like they did with Joseph in the Bible. None of his siblings believed in his dreams.

As a goal digger, be firm about your life plan. Anyone you share your plans with should contribute to your development and support you. If they do not, take no notice of their discouraging habits.

FRIENDSHIP

You definitely cannot be friends with a person at your level. The disadvantage of being friends with your peers physically and psychologically is that you beat around one and the same things every day. Life is all about hobbies and not life goals.

I like the story of David and Jonathan in the Bible. Jonathan was born into a royal family with his father, Solomon, standing as a wise and respected king. David learned how a king treats himself,   and the traits of a king, and the tools he needed to rule. He ended up becoming a king, even though he was not born into kingship.

The disadvantage of choosing your peer, as a friend, makes you more emotional than strategic.

You always want to keep up with their feelings and mood swings. You want a sense of belonging and always compromise your life plans to meet their friendship expectations, such as clubbing and sporting.

If you put your friends before you, you become vulnerable. Putting someone else in front of your future or before your purpose weakens your judgement, kills your ambition and dims your future. Be your own man.

MENTORSHIP

If you are a girl, and your boyfriend in an argument says, "My mother said . . ." just let it go. You are fighting an impossible battle.

This goes to mentors who always tell you how others did things without showing you how to get things done by yourself. Such mentors are very dangerous because they will delay your growth.

You will spend time reading about heroes instead of working toward your own heroism. A mentor should be someone who learns about your life purpose and is willing to take you through it.

Jesus did not tell Peter about the possibility of walking on the water. He walked on water and called Peter to follow him. That's mentorship, helping you do things you thought you could never do.

Today, Peter is the cornerstone of Jesus's ministry and has done even greater things. Choose a mentor who can make things happen for you. Mentorship is not a theoretical process, and it is nothing but practice.

Read more about mentorship, its advantages and disadvantages, and related scenarios in Chapter Five (Fifth Piece). There you will also be guided on how to pick up a mentor and when to leave that mentorship.

ENTREPRENEURSHIP

At this stage, many feel they can do anything to achieve what they want. They see entrepreneurship as solution to everything.

The energy is high and the mind is money-driven. It pains me to realise that many people, especially youngsters, think starting a business without a plan will help them escape poverty.

Some confuse a company registration with a business. I will deliberate more on this in chapter five where I give a guide for successful entrepreneurship and getting started with or without funding.

DICTATORSHIP

This stage comes to its natural conclusion once your vision is realised. People feel old, worn out and come to the realisation that they have accomplished everything they could accomplish in their life.

This stage of life is centred on the creation of legacy.

When DJ Sbu wore his brand and drank his brand on a national television, he knew he was in conflict of interest. All he wanted to do was to show the world and his employers that his ambition was bigger than taking instruction from anybody.

Same happened to Tbo Touch when he started imposing his own features in his show at Metro FM. He treated his producer with temerity and effectively making the person redundant, which is remaining for the sake of filling a post. Touch's actions came from his own head rather than from the script.

In short, at this stage, you should have beaten or surpassed all the odds. You have gathered every resource to do anything you ever wanted, just to set the standard higher. You only dictate on your beliefs and plans because you have gathered resources and can afford to be on your own.

Some people get to this stage without a backbone. As a result, their dreams die a natural death. They spend their savings on unrewarding choices.

First Piece: Is The Glass Half Full Or Half Empty?

WHAT HAPPENS IN THIS STAGE	WHY DO YOU GET STUCK	HOW TO MOVE ON
Financial pressure	Spending money on depreciating goods	Invest in property
Eager to settle down	Fear of committing	Commit to one person
Force your advice upon others	Pride without learning	Learn from others
Family pressure	Feeling obligated	Draw boundaries
In need of career development	Undermine current job	Work hard, get recognition
Confusion	Undecided priorities	Prioritise
Rapid Changes	Resist change	Change for the better
Hunger for power begins to haunt you	Arrogance	Respect, be humble and learn
Philanthropy	Working alone, selfish	Work positively with others
You don't take instruction	Pride	Learn from others

Second Piece

I Am

Who am I anyway?

I am not a product of my circumstances. I am a product of my decisions – Stephen Covey.

OPEN

1. Are you not ashamed of yourself at this moment?
2. Do you believe in your future as you have planned for it?

DIGEST

1. If you were to reverse any moment, what would it be? Why?

RELATE

1. When last did you look at an opportunity and decided to let it pass, despite qualifying?
2. Do you feel less qualified sometimes when you look at your counterparts?

About the piece

This should be your mantra for leading a more responsible life where the things you say are the things you wish for and to do. This chapter looks at the concept "I AM" to help the reader that it all begins with taking responsibility and building courage and confidence. Never undermine or be undermined by someone, or yourself, at the beginning of the journey or life race just because someone is ahead. Their journey might end up at your mercy. Imagine you are a teacher who hated a certain child at school and bedridden as you are, you are told that doctor so and so is the only specialist in the country who can bring you back to life. This chapter prepares you to take responsibility of your actions, your journey in order to discover your purpose. Purpose is like gold, you don't find it lying around. Dig it. The keyword is I AM and not I AM NOT. Now that you found yourself in the first chapter as you assessed your situation, it should be easy to say "I Am" going forward.

People can judge you but they cannot sentence you – Deekay Maria Makgoba.

I can do everything through Him who gives me strength – Philippians 4:13

35

The other day, I woke up to a motivation session on Facebook. I posted about ten back-to-back motivational quotes as I thought of them. A lot of my Facebook friends were wondering what got into me because I flooded their timeline early in the morning. It was unlike what they used to read from me. One even asked if I'd eaten cereals that day. Truth is that I was saddened by how people can declare impossibilities in their lives.

I had sent several job ads to an unemployed friend, who texted me back and said: "Thank you for the heads up." But then she said she was not the perfect fit. She said that she didn't have the required experience. She said the last time she tried – everything fell apart. She was like many people: capable but unemployed.

That was when I realised that the phrase I AM NOT has stolen many dreams. Instead of selling yourself, telling people about what you can do, all you do is broadcast your own weaknesses, flaws and imprecisions.

If this resonates with you, it's about time for you to take a stand and say: I may not have done it before, but I know I can do it. Every job that can be seen today was done for the first time by a person who was inexperienced and unqualified. Learn the secret of being content in every situation, whether well fed or hungry, whether living in a shack or a double storey, whether educated or not, whether confident or anxious. Never give in to your doubt.

If you believe that God created you in his image, you will believe that whatever you confess with your mouth will manifest. When God created heaven and earth, he used the word. You, too, whatever you say shall become. If all you have to say is I AM NOT, you will never live your life to the fullest.

Let me tell you about many people who thought they were not good enough in life. People who thought their lives amounted to nothing great. When God sent Moses to release the Israelites, all Moses could do was to belittle himself. He weakened himself. He described himself as an underdog. He thought he was a pathetic man. He saw himself as good enough only in the bushes as a shepherd.

In Exodus 3: 13, Moses asked God what he should tell the people when they asked who sent him. Moses said to God, "Who am I, that I should go to Pharaoh and bring the Israelites out of Egypt?" God told him that whatever he was going to do, or any question he will come across, he should tell them that it was I who sent him. God told Moses to say: "I am who I am. I am has sent me to you."

Before you were born, God has set you aside. God has made you uniquely different. God gave you the power to make the best out of your life. Start to stop saying you are not. Defeat your fears and try something new today.

Start to stop saying you are not.

Take responsibility and say you are who you think you are. You are a winner. You are better in the future. You are something that is beyond comparison.

Second Piece: I Am

Fingerprints develop at the time of conception. And fingerprints are matchless, even those of identical twins. So, you are what your fingerprint says you are – different and irreplaceable. You were born exclusive.

Put your self-doubt aside. After all, you've got nothing to lose when you give yourself a chance at what you want to achieve. When you look at the people who are glorious today, it's easy to assume they've all had luck, favour, fortune, support, and money handed to them on a silver platter.

In Grade 12, there was this guy who understood mathematics better than the rest of the class. He came from a rich family or so it seemed. He had a computer while the rest of us did not own a *vula-vala* or sliding cell phone. When the maths teacher was not around, he would leave him with a textbook to teach us.

He obtained all totals in the year. He typed assignments when the rest of us wrote by pen. He would get high marks for presenting neat work. We all confidently assumed that he was blessed with the right genes, born with talent and diligence.

Nevertheless, at the end of the year, I got better grades in maths and went on to pass with a bachelor whereas he passed with a diploma and could not get to his dream university. He repeated the grade and produced the same result.

Second Piece: I Am

In life, we rise and fall. Life is about singing praises to yourself even when the going gets tough. The most important thing is that you are going.

George Foreman once told himself that he wanted to be the champion of the world when it came to boxing but he was defeated, and put into retirement. Ten years later, he decided to get back into the ring. He was fifty pounds overweight and a laughing stock whom hardly anyone took seriously. When he regained the title at 45, he became the oldest heavyweight champion in history.

Foreman did not say I cannot make it because I am too old. He did not worry about the humiliation he would have suffered had he lost again. He was not concerned about being beaten twice. But he cared about getting what he wanted.

God often places our success in the middle of nowhere, sometimes in a valley of trouble. You have to be vigilant to see it coming. You have to be strong to push away anything that stops you from his glory.

You might be measuring your success against that of your peers. You might undervalue your capabilities when you see how excellent they are. You might see no future as life throws tantrums at you. You might quit when things don't look promising.

In the race of life, the requirements, strategy and tactics differ from one person to the other. So, the last will be first, and the first will be last or otherwise.

Second Piece: I Am

In the Bible, a landowner went out early in the morning to hire workers for his vineyard. He agreed to pay them one silver coin for the day and sent them into his vineyard.

About nine in the morning he hired others.

About noon and about three in the afternoon he hired more workers.

About five in the afternoon he did the same.

When evening came, the owner of the vineyard sent his foreman to go and call the workers and pay them their wages, beginning with the last ones hired and going on to the first.

The workers who were hired about five in the afternoon came and each received a coin. So, those who were hired first at nine in the morning expected to receive more. But each one of them also received a coin. When they received it, they began to grumble against the landowner, saying those who were hired last worked only one hour. They were not happy to have received equal pay after their long, hard work and enduring the heat of the day.

Life is unpredictable. Life is personal. Life is yours to live. People around you only add to your life purpose but never dictate to it. Do not compare your journey with others. God might put you last to bless you first.

Like education, we all start the same way, taught the same things, get the same hours to attend, break at the same time and are taught by the same people. But the ultimate prize of education is personal. Engineers started the same way as teachers, and teachers taught engineers. Engineers invented the teaching material, and planned and designed teaching places such as schools etc. In your own opinion, who has ran a better race between the two – a teacher and an engineer?

Your race is God's plan to serve the world. It is not a competition that leads to pressure, jealousy, hatred and temptations. It is easy to fall when you run your race looking sideways. The prize of your race is never on the grand stand but ahead. Put your mind and your eyes ahead. That is what we call focus.

In a race, you get tired. Your eyes swell. Your hope decreases. But courage is your fuel, keep it full. Only in the dark you can see the stars, shining so brightly. You might think the lights of your future are dimming, but sometimes things are clearer, richer, and purer when everyone else is focused on what they want. Your purpose will never be clear if you want it to look like that of someone else.

The best way to believe you can do something is when you do it.

"Hope is like a road in the country; there was never a road, but when many people walk on it, the road comes into existence," Lin Yutang.

In scriptures, Hannah held on to the one thing she wanted in life. She knew she has done all things right. You may have studied the right degree. You may have fulfilled all the requirements and remain jobless.

Hannah was married to Elkanah who had another wife called Peninnah. Peninnah had children while Hannah remained barren. They did not start together as wives; Hannah was the primary wife. But later in life, Hannah bore a son called Samuel. God had closed her womb. God knew that Hannah's son will have more purpose. He had to come last in order to help those who came first.

Our dreams are never denied, delayed, distracted or late. We humans just want them before their actual time. We are late to start and get ahead too fast.

Today, things may not be possible for you. Things may work against your will. You may lose respect for you are deemed useless. But God will deliver you. You are born with a purpose. You are born to produce something precious that will outshine your neighbour. Something valuable that will last forever. Something special that will be admired by everyone. Something great that will surpass human understanding. Something awesome that will give hope to the world. Something wonderful that everyone will wish for.

God will be God tomorrow. Don't be anxious. Don't doubt yourself. Don't underestimate yourself. Don't lose sight of your strength. Even a strong man gets weak. Believe that you can do it. Ignore your fears.

Pray for your worry. Nothing in all making, except your fears, can detach you from your goal.

We have all been frustrated by the way people treated us. We have equally contributed to someone's pain. We have all been confused somewhere, somehow. We have all had distraction and discomfort in life. We all suffered embarrassment at some point in life. From all these things, we have been redeemed by Christ.

Someone is called useless in their marriage but are the last hope to others. Someone is called useless in their workplace but are a valuable breadwinner to their families. Someone is a useless singer but a comforter to someone. Lift your chin higher and stop comparing yourself to people you don't even know how they succeeded.

Acknowledge yourself. All your thoughts and capabilities exist as you allow them to exist. If you think you are not good enough to master maths at school, you will never be a doctor or an engineer. If you think you are not gifted to win a race, you will never enter any race. Everything you will experience is a product of your thoughts and beliefs. Let your daily experiences help you discover that you have inherited awesome gifts of creating from God.

There is that little thing that makes you exceptional; you will only uncover it once you start stopping to think you are not good enough.

Zacchaeus ran ahead of everyone and climbed a sycamore-fig tree to see Jesus. He knew he could not see given the flock in front of him, and obviously many of them were taller than him. He accepted that he was shorter than almost everyone in the crowd. He had to make a plan to get what he wanted. He had to defeat the thought that he couldn't make it. God empowers people who try their level best.

Once you are ready to help yourself, no one, and nothing, can stop you.

The first chapter of this book, and the longest, tried to show you how responsible you are in every situation. I AM is a transition from that chapter. You will only make the best out of your situations if you put aside blame and decide to make the best out of that situation.

If you convince yourself that you cannot do something without someone's help, you will never do it. Unfortunately, usually people help you when it is beneficial to them. It's what is in for me.

Should it not be beneficial, they will leave you halfway or drop you just like that. The reason the blind man stayed besides the well of life for so many years is that he was promised to be taken in by someone.

That someone took him from home to the well, but decided to leave him lying there. A mission based on others never lasts because it has no foundation and guarantees. The blind man could have just rolled inside the water, but he wanted someone to do it for him.

Many people say I AM NOT instead of I AM because they think one has to live preciously in order to make it in life.

There would not be any school dropouts or thieves in life if we all knew that success is like a treasure hidden in the field, you need to find it while you work the field, often by chance.

Second Piece: I Am

*The following passage, or seven ideas, are the elements of achievement – **S**chool, **U**nderstand, **C**ourage, **C**hange, **E**xplore, **S**upport, and **S**tandout. This is a SUCCESS MODEL. Each initial letter, combined makes up success.*

SCHOOL – *The only constant in successful people is the ability to learn, as you educate yourself, about your own talents.* By school I am not talking about the building where we are inspired to forget about ourselves and become aware of the hopes and needs of our parents, neighbours, and everybody. Successful people had self-discovery as their starting point.

UNDERSTAND – If you can find it in your heart to accept that the physical building is not a school, you will have time to understand what you can do, and not what others did. That which you can do must drive you to do the extraordinary, to challenge yourself. Once you follow your heart, you will realise that passion is the heart of your courage.

COURAGE – Unfortunately, successful people are never sure of what courage is, no wonder they keep on looking for it until their death. This is simply because one achievement serves as courage for the next, up to endlessness. Courage doesn't always roar. Sometimes it is the little voice at the end of the day that says, *"I'll try again tomorrow."* This is the ability not to do anything in the world but to do everything for the world.

CHANGE – Once you have courage about your passion, you will have a set of new priorities and change comes by default. Lord Chesterfield once said, *"Man cannot discover new oceans unless he has the courage to lose sight of the shore."*

EXPLORE – A change will mean one thing – expand your horizons by letting go of the familiar. No man can achieve greatness unless he sees all that is around him as ordinary. Many challenges you face in your journey to success are most likely caused by the past. Exploring simply means you stop benchmarking because your dream is not meant to be a duplicate. But going for new things will require a massive support.

SUPPORT – Be willing to ask for help. To be crazy about your passion or having courage to do anything does not make you an iron man. It is through people that you can realise your full potential. As they either support or disapprove your ideas, you get to learn how to be better than them. Standing out from the rest is your ticket to being anything you want to be, anywhere.

STAND OUT – Being different from ordinary people is the best feeling in the world. By then, or should you get to a point where you feel this way, know that you have made it through to the last step – success. You would have made it in life.

Third Piece

Status Changes You

It's all in the {Attitude}

About the piece

OPEN

1. Do you want to change?
2. Have you ever felt that as if you want to change but you do not know what needs to change?

DIGEST

1. If you were to change now, what would be the change?
2. Does your environment allow for change or is it holding you back?

RELATE

1. When last did you experience change in your life? How did it affect other people?

A blind girl hated herself just because she was blind. She hated everyone, except her loving boyfriend. He was always there for her. She said that if she could only see the world, she would marry her boyfriend. One day, someone donated a pair of eyes to her and then she could see everything, including her boyfriend. Her boyfriend asked her, "Now that you can see the world, will you marry me?" The girl was shocked when she saw that her boyfriend was blind too, and refused to marry him. Her boyfriend walked away in tears, and later wrote a letter to her: "Just take care of my eyes, dear."

This chapter is a twin sister to the previous one. Now that you have identified your situation and accepted responsibility that change begins with you, you have to change. You did some of the things you did because a particular situation dictated them. Now it's your chance. People change for three reasons: They have learned a lot. They have suffered enough. They got tired of always doing the same thing. This piece hopes to teach you to anticipate greater changes in your life. A status is like wind, it changes direction, at any time.

50

Third Piece: Status Changes You

One of the saddest things to realise is that certain people are just not who they used to be, the people who you once considered best friends. They are now, at best, strangers.

It's not that there's been any major falling out or pivotal movement when a friendship changed, but as C.S. Lewis so eloquently put it: "Isn't it funny how day by day nothing changes, but when you look back, everything is different?"

What we have learnt from the blind girl in the introduction is how the human brain changes when the status changes.

Only a few remember what life was before, and who's always been there even in the most painful situations. Some want credit for the things they have done out of love, and some think they have contributed to your success even though they did not.

I remember when one of my friends, Arthur Masoma, affectionately known as Mr Flamboyant, bought a car. He had a lot of friends who helped him during his hustling times. But his ultimate success was not an effort to be nationalised. It was only a few who took him to higher places. One insulted him on Facebook, labelling him an ungrateful b***h. Some wanted him to report to them whenever he was driving to certain places. Some said the car changed him, and, by that time, the car was a week-old. Some felt like he had to show them the car before everyone else.

Third Piece: Status Changes You

It was an emotional fiasco.

Above all, truth is that life is a gift. We all have to move to the next level at some point, even if it means leaving others in the previous phase. We cannot be friends forever. I sound like Julius Malema now. *Hehehe*! I didn't mean to laugh like President Zuma, sorry.

It is only fair when your success does not change your heart: it only changes your mind. As they say, do not look down upon others unless you are helping them to get out a tough situation.

Do not strike back at those who think you have changed and see them as nothing. It is an egoistic talking. Their ego will be wounded and recover as a matter of time. Give them time and space to comprehend that you have taken a different step in life. This means the people who were there for you will never be forgotten in your life.

As soon as you want to move on without the people who were there for you, then you never had them in your heart. You just had them in your corner.

In life, there are friends, associates and acquaintances; and everyone is there for a purpose. People come into your life for different reasons at different times. Some may help you through a difficult period; others are there to stay as lifelong friends or partners. Learn to recognise the difference and let those who have passed their expiration date carry on their journey without you.

7 Ways To Deal With Change In People, Otherwise, There's Nothing You Can Do

1. Figure out who you are without them.

2. Distinguish between what you want to do and what you felt obligated to do.

3. Stop helping people when it's hurting you, just know that the lessons these people teach are more valuable than the people.

4. Establish that your time line isn't the same as theirs.

5. Realise that judging others is a waste of your time and you will understand that they may not be who they used to be, but neither are you.

6. Accept that some people were meant to be in your life for a moment, not a lifetime.

7. Learn when people are being fake so you can teach yourself to be more real, and have one real friend rather than 100 fake ones.

7 Quotes To Make You Accept Change,
whether in you or in others:

To improve is to change; to be perfect is to change often.

- Winston Churchill

Any change, even a change for the better, is always accompanied by drawbacks and discomforts.

- Arnold Bennett

Change your thoughts and you change your   world.

- Norman Vincent Peale

If you don't like something, change it. If you can't change it, change your attitude.

-   Maya Angelou

Change is the law of life. And those who look only to the past or present are certain to miss the   future.

- John F. Kennedy

The first step toward change is awareness. The second step is acceptance.

- Nathaniel Branden

You cannot control what happens to you, but you   can control your attitude toward what happens to you, and in that, you will be mastering change rather than allowing it to master you.

- Brian Tracy

Peace of mind comes from not wanting to change   others.

- Gerald Jampolsky

Karma
has no menu. You get served what you deserve.

Although we have to change, it is better to have a positive change. A positive change is a result of improved social skills, satisfactory attitude and better thinking. It is unescapable that change will always affect people around you. We move on with other people and without others. It is advisable, nonetheless, to never mess with karma. Do right by people as you move to the next level in life. Today, before you think of saying an unkind word – think of someone who can't speak. No matter how successful you can become, you will always need people.

7 RULES OF *BEFORE*

How to change without hurting others, deliberately

1. *Before* you complain about the taste of your food – think of someone who has nothing to eat.

2. *Before* you complain about your husband or wife – think of someone who is crying out to God for a companion.

3. *Before* you think of pointing the finger or condemning another – remember that not one of us are without fault.

4. *Before* you complain about your children – think of someone who desires children but they're barren.

5. *Before* you argue about your dirty house, someone didn't clean or sweep – think of the people who are living in the streets.

6. *Before* whining about the distance you drive – think of someone who walks the same distance.

7. *Before* you complain about your job – think of the unemployed, the disabled and those who wished they had your job.

If you will not remember the *BEFORE* Rule, better recall the THINK Rule:

*T*rue? *H*elpful? *I*nspiring? *N*ecessary? *K*ind?

Third Piece: Status Changes You

People want change, but they don't want to change

Now that you have learned to shape your belief system, I believe your glass is half-full.

You have come a long way.

You have done so many things you never thought you were capable of. Yes, YOU CAN! Start taking charge of your life and change your life.

Say I AM in every situation to avoid blaming and complaining about your situation. You benefit not from blaming someone when things go wrong, but by taking responsibility and seeking change.

Question how it all went wrong if you were there and knew some things were just wrong.

Shifting responsibility is the sharpest razor you can ever use to cut yourself short.

See the bigger picture

Seven Things To Learn About Risk

To live is to risk dying.

To try is to risk failure.

To hope is to risk despair.

To laugh is to risk appearing foolish.

To weep is to risk appearing sentimental.

To love is to risk not being loved in return.

To reach out for another is to risk involvement.

To expose feelings is to risk exposing your true self.

To place your ideas or your dreams before a crowd is to risk their loss.

Third Piece: Status Changes You

When you want to join a picture or a jigsaw puzzle together, you have to see the bigger picture. Putting together a picture puzzle is very challenging but it can easily be put together when you follow clues.

You need to see the picture which is obviously unseen by people who do not know what you want to achieve.

When you put it together, you are sure that there is a complete picture, but in the beginning, all you can see are pieces that do not even look promising. This is called vision.

To solve a puzzle, you should firstly look for an area where no one will mix up your pieces, whether by accident or intentionally.

Ensure that your area is big enough to accommodate the picture you have in mind.

Turn all pieces face up so you can start grouping similar colours together.

Start joining similar colours, eventually you will realise that filling gaps is even easier.

Success is like that. You need to take baby steps to get to the top. A baby obviously takes time to reach their destination.

Third Piece: Status Changes You

Give Yourself Enough Time To finish

The worst form of self-sabotage is to think you are running out of time. Such stress happens to people who don't have time at all. Having time does not mean you are free.

It means working on a schedule you set for your goals. So many people start one project and shift to another before completing the first one.

They would think about a third project before the second takes shape. Such people are pressured by their own fears and would never learn to do things the right way. They run a race they clearly know they won't finish.

Engaging in many activities at once will only create a conflict of ideas, a tired body, a confused plan, leading to what we call *time-crunch-stress* – you feel pressed for time but you are yet to make a significant progress.

Stop glorifying being busy. Work on one thing at a time and do not do it for Instagram posts.

Those who pretend to be busy often do it to frustrate the enemy they do not even know or have for that matter.

As you learn to finish projects, you open doors for bigger projects and your life will change, along with your status.

Third Piece: Status Changes You

Prepared but never ready

In my first year, I had quite a number of friends from each subject I took. We would group for presentations. My dear friend, Marema Mokhosana, would sound more than prepared during discussions, so we nominated him to present in class. But on the last day, he would start giving us excuses.

Karabo Matlala and Sontaga Letshelele would do the same. At first, I thought they were not prepared due to being scared or shy.

However, I soon realised that they were prepared, for we would have gone through the content together. That's when I realised that they were prepared but not ready to deliver the preparations. In most cases, I was nominated to present.

Today, the above-mentioned are presenters of note. They don't need to be ready to deliver what they prepare as current affairs hosts and producers on Thobela FM. They get ready as they prepare. They know the content by heart and not by chance. Their status around presenting has totally changed and no one changed it but themselves.

This is how successful people are supposed to be, getting ready on the go. If you ever find yourself wanting something so much but without courage to go after it, success becomes undefined.

The moment you drag your feet, success fades away and becomes elusive.

So many bits will fade away until success becomes uncertain just like in the case of a beautiful woman who takes her time looking for Mr Right.

Normally, when she finds him, the man would show his rightness by asking for her hand in marriage. And you would be surprised when the lady rejects the proposal on the grounds that she's "not ready."

How do you prepare for Mr Right if you are not going to take him off the market?

Not being ready often lets success pass you by, the one right thing you have been waiting for.

When you change your attitude, your status changes. When you make up your mind, your status changes.

Do not feel bad when it is time to change how things used to be. Change is personal and inevitable. But taking too long to change might make the change not such a success — by the time you'd finished with all your shilly-shallyings.

Move on and stop moving around

The best feeling ever in the whole world, I think even in heaven, is watching things finally fall into place after seeing them fall apart over a long time.

People who do not have purpose in life are the busiest. Let me give an example of the difference between moving on and moving around.

There was a certain girl in my village who was well known to be incapable of saying no to men. She would date friends and not give a care in the world.

One day, during free period in class, she fought with another girl over a boyfriend.

As they exchanged words, she said: "I moved on from that stupid boy of yours. I am now dating Tshepo."

When I looked at Tshepo, and her other exes, there were more similarities than differences. All her exes were drunkards, less educated if not uneducated, and bums.

That's when I realised the difference between moving on and moving around. When she was talking, I could see images of kids on some roundabout at a public park.

All they do is move around and feel like they are moving to somewhere. But the fact is after the moving is done, one lands at the same place, right on the first spot.

I warn against trying to be a jack-of-all-trades without mastering a particular one.

One runs the risk of dying poor without acquiring certain skills.

You cannot be a soccer player, a singer, a CEO, a community developer and so on.

Some will suffer. Rather create things and leave them for others to keep alive. People will always remember you as the creator.

Credit will forever be yours. Who cares who's on the Facebook Team? Create followers by not overstaying in one project. That's moving on. On to greater heights, of course.

Fourth Piece

MENTORSHIP

OPEN

About the piece

1. Do you believe in mentorship? Why?
2. Ever had a mentor? How did things go?
3. What are advantages of mentorship? Disadvantages?

DIGEST

1. If you were to be a mentor now, how would you conduct your sessions?

RELATE

1. You are given a task to appoint two mentors for a certain programme, how are you going to pick them out of hundreds applications?

Being a great person in life is difficult, and trying to do bigger and greater things is even worse.

Attempting to do greater things alone is close to impossible. That is why all great leaders have mentors, and mentor others.

No matter how intelligent, competitive, and resourced one may be— particularly early in your career – success is, in reality, a group effort.

Mentorship is a key driver of success.

The trick is finding the right mentor(s). This chapter will help you understand the importance of mentorship as well as its advantages and disadvantages.

Fourth Piece: Mentorship

You are never too successful to need a mentor

There are some people who are too proud and think they have all what it takes to reach their full potential without the help of a mentor.

Most of them are afraid to face the real world. They are afraid to unveil their weaknesses to other people. They are scared to fail in front of others.

They are ashamed to admit that they need help. They are uncertain about their dreams and aspirations.

No one is born with the ability to overcome the world and its challenges. It takes someone who came before to show others the way.

That is a mentor. Not that a mentor is something out of the ordinary. He or she is only an experienced person who happens to be active in your field.

Steve Jobs had Bill Campbell as a mentor; Mark Zuckerberg had Steve Jobs; Bill Gates had Warren Buffett.

Fourth Piece: Mentorship

What a mentor is, and how to pick one

Before you start looking for a mentor, know what it is that you want to achieve. A mentor will not help you think about what you want in life.

A mentor is there to sharpen your thinking and turn it into reality.

If you ever ask to be mentored, you are likely to be rejected. Mentors are interested in hard workers. The relationship often starts with a shared passion.

Mentors often select mentees based on their performance and potential.

So, shift your thinking from "If I get a mentor, I'll excel", to "If I excel, I'll get a mentor." The trick is to identify a mentor and volunteer in their projects or pitch ideas to them.

In addition, look for someone who has achieved greatness and has mutual desire.

Beware of people who specialise in lip service. They are not mentors but spectators and commentators at the same time. A mentor should teach you how to do things and not tell you how other people did things.

I have seen this in most individuals who engage in motivational speaking. Having information about how things are supposed to be done does not qualify one to be a mentor.

Don't fall for their smooth talk and charm. *They are just talking too much – to hide their struggles in life.*

Mentorship does not come with an age tag attached to it. Anyone can be a mentor. But it's very hard for an 18-year-old to be a mentor, because mentorship is all about experience, both personal and professional.

The bottom line is knowledge, application, connection and leadership.

What to look for when choosing a mentor

- **The Challenger,** who asks questions about why your comfort zone is the way it is, until it no longer exists.

- **The Cheerleader,** who relentlessly boosts your self-esteem and confidence until you feel brave enough to step over your own boundaries.

- **The Coach,** who is a wizened veteran providing the knowledge you need to innovate – or overcome the same adversities he conquered.

Fourth Piece: Mentorship

Perseverance is the only constant in mentorship

When I started writing, I received guidance from a mentor who was a writer. I saw an advert seeking student writers for a new student magazine, Keyaka. I applied like everybody else, but what set me apart was my curiosity to learn more than writing.

Metji Makgoba was the project leader who conceptualised the whole magazine from the scratch through guidance of his boss. The way I bothered him, he ended up preferring me over other applicants who were honours and master's students. I was only in the first semester of my second year of media studies.

His knowledge of writing was exactly what I needed to kick-start a career in writing. That was my passion. I read his writings and felt he was the kind of a writer I could follow.

He threw me under the bus by appointing me as the first editor. He then fired me before I could start with my role because I missed one meeting. I was replaced in that meeting.

When I considered how I planned the content of the magazine with him, looking for names and deciding on what to cover, I got mad and gave him a piece of my mind. Metji is very critical and sensitive and it was sometimes hard to work with him.

He was a perfectionist who could sometimes be mistaken for someone who is self-centered. He handled the whole project very well but I felt he took a hasty decision when he fired me.

Today, we joke about it and he admits that sacking me was wrong considering that I was very committed from the beginning. After our heated conversation, which I must say I was very emotional, he reconsidered his decision and told me that he needed someone who is serious about the role because the future of the magazine depended on the editor.

He never doubted my abilities and was very encouraging throughout my writing career. He would read my work, send me books to sharpen my craft and reminded me that if I need to grow as a writer, I need to write regularly.

Because I worked hard and demonstrated that I was indeed paying attention to his counsel, he did not hesitate to recommend me to my employ that I was a good writer.

I also have to add that Metji was not very old. He was 22 when we started the magazine but he was already more mature because he was mentored by an English professor, Dr Rosemary McCabe, writers Hosea Ramphekwa and Elijah Moholola. His writing was impressive from the start and he has a strong command of the language.

Because I knew that he was capable and understood that I could learn from his experience, I did not allow his weaknesses as a person to spoil our relationship. I did not let his attitude and my pride stand before my dream of mastering the art of writing.

But our experience together has taught me many things about mentorship. Throughout our interactions, I realised that Metji was not comfortable speaking in front of people.

At that time, because of my activities at school, church, and other community engagements, I had already developed decent public speaking skills.

I started encouraging him to speak more in public and invited him to speak during some of our student events. His gift, with more exposure and actions, developed and he is now very comfortable to deliver public presentations.

He does political and sports analysis on radio and a lecturer and a senior student in media and cultural studies. Metji knew his weaknesses and that he was not comfortable with public speaking.

Despite him being my supervisor at the magazine project, he did not doubt that my experience could help develop his own gift. He allowed me to intervene.

A mentor can make or break you.

Personally, I have met an influx of students and loafers who came to me looking for a mentor. Some did not ask me directly. I just read their minds.

One day, three young girls came to my office oozing confidence and full of energy. They passionately spoke about a business idea they had just developed.

But when they pitched their concept to me, I realised that their work was a duplicate of a certain concept. They had plagiarised.

I frankly told them that business is mainly an idea that identifies a gap in the market and fills it. The idea has to address that need. I told them that theirs was a duplicate and cannot be regarded as a business idea but a copy of a certain concept. They left and never came back.

One of those girls happens to be one of my mentees today. Relotegile Malepe did not use the first encounter as the end of her learning. She is doing perfectly fine.

Had she stopped believing in mentorship the day I told them that their concept needed reworking, she would not be one of the best today.

When you look for a mentor, learn to accept and give feedback. With mentorship, honesty is always crucial. One of the hardest things in mentorship is constructive criticism.

Many of us find it difficult to give people feedback in a sincere way.

We fall into the trap of using harsh words, which effectively discourages the mentee. Your mentees can sometimes, just like interns, produce a mediocre piece of work.

Since mentorship is a process, it is important to avoid using emotive language that could leave them dejected and discouraged. It is hard to internalise feedback, and to act on its instruction, if we feel it is overly negative.

Helping someone develop his or her talent is not easy but we try to make it smooth. Equally, as a mentee, you should learn to approach feedback with an open mind.

Having people who comment on your work with the intention of nourishing and harnessing your talent is priceless. It requires time, efforts and resources.

Things get worse for those of us who read negative feedback as a challenge or an insult.

Having a mentor means, you are literally asking someone to criticise you all the time.

Fourth Piece: Mentorship

Play comes before work only in the dictionary

Real mentors are very sensitive and often come across as rude. This is because they don't have time to catch up and talk about useless stuff. Mentors, equally, do not like to be associated with dumb mentees.

Do not be too comfortable. Don't ask a question when you can find the answer yourself. You need to have challenges to overcome. The mentor needs to focus on your progress, rather not your excuses.

Be ready to move on

Do not accept the roles that society foists on you. Re-create yourself by forging a new identity, one that commands attention and never bores the audience. Be the master of your own image rather than letting others define it for you. Incorporate dramatic devices into your public gestures and actions – your power will be enhanced and your character will seem larger than life.

- by Robert Greene and Joost Elffers.

Sometimes mentees come out as shadows of their mentors. They are identical in how they conduct themselves, speak, and view the world. But it is important to be independent during the mentorship process and develop your own identity.

Fourth Piece: Mentorship

Be true to your dreams and have the desire to develop something new. Mentorship is not to teach us conformity. Your first mentor might only be of help in the beginning phase.

To grow, you will have to move on to the next level, which means you have to find a new mentor.

Mentorship might limit your thinking if you end up believing you cannot do anything without your mentor. We should not fall into a trap of seeking validation from our mentors all the time. The question of faith becomes crucial in the case.

While it is important to learn from other people, we have to learn to embrace our own uniqueness and seek to fly without seeking to please other people.

And some mentors are more emotional than others. You might find he or she wants to be acknowledged all the time for contributing to your development.

But you won't lose anything by letting them feel important. Even when your mentor might seem self-important, appreciate his contribution in your life.

There is nothing more fulfilling to any teacher than seeing their students challenge the status quo, and finding ways to contribute new, fresh ideas to a subject with passion and purpose.

This pleases teachers because they can see that their efforts have not been in vain.

What they have taught has not only been understood, but has been expanded. Metaphorically-speaking, it is a giver's desire that their generosity is rewarded in this way.

When teaching, we not only expect students to master the academic literature and take ownership of the content but we also expect them to identify gaps and search for alternatives.

Students, who memorise the content parrot-fashion without deducing something from it, defeat the whole point of learning and teaching, no matter how good their grades.

Institutions need to be on their guard to identify and help students who are still resorting to memorising content because they lack the confidence and skills to process it into knowledge.

Exposing students to critical theories and academic literature is not enough, or does not seek to condition their minds.

Rather, it seeks to provide them with a solid foundation with which they can develop the confidence to question and to unleash their creativity.

We are looking to develop innovators, trailblazers and intellects who are at home in their field but restlessly seek to improve it.

The only important thing is to know when it is time to move to the next level. No man is a jack-of-all-trades.

Your success is a combination of various expertise – mentors – in different areas. But the biggest rule is to build trust with all your mentors.

You will receive favour

You may remember that I said that honesty is very crucial. Mentors go beyond mentorship and advocate for their mentees. But no one can put in a good word for something they are not sure about. Being honest means clearly discussing your career goals with your mentor. Your mentor can simply endorse you on social media such as LinkedIn, for the skills they taught you. They introduce you to their network and open doors for you.

men☺or

ADVISER | FRIEND | TUTOR | TEACHER | COACH | GUIDE

CHANGE THE ODDS. **BE A MENTOR.**

In this context, trust is very important. Don't be an unpredictable mentee who does not know what they want. You should learn to focus on developing one skill at a time. Your mentor can only introduce you to the real world, create opportunities and connections when they know what is important and useful to you. They would not know if you keep on changing your mind about what you want to do.

A mentor needs to trust that you are reliable. To build trust, you should always follow their counsel and put concerted efforts in your work. Consistency will help you build trust with your mentor.

THE GREATEST GIFT YOU CAN GIVE *Yourself* IS YOUR TIME.

BECAUSE WHEN YOU GIVE YOUR TIME, YOU ARE GIVING A PORTION OF YOUR LIFE THAT YOU WILL NEVER GET BACK.

Fifth Piece

The Important Things In Life

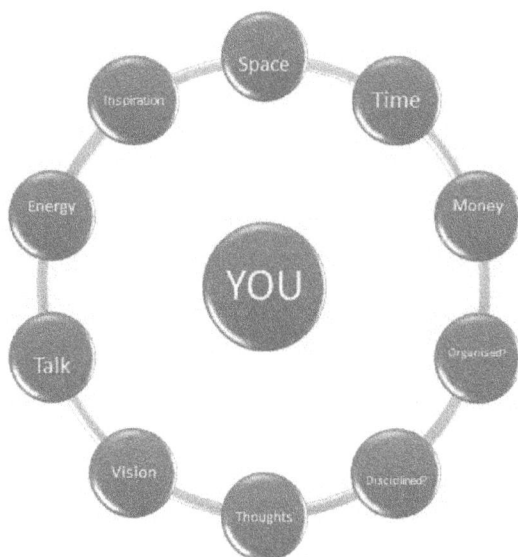

Fifth Piece: The Important Things In Life

About the piece

A philosophy professor stood before his class with some items on the table in front of him. When the class began, he picked up a very large and empty mayonnaise jar and proceeded to fill it with stones, about 2 inches in diameter.

He then asked the students if the jar was full. They agreed that it was.

So the professor then picked up a box of pebbles and poured them into the jar. He shook the jar lightly. The pebbles, of course, rolled into the open areas between the stones.

He then asked the students again if the jar was full. They agreed it was. The professor picked up a box of sand and poured it into the jar. Of course, the sand filled up the remaining open areas of the jar.

He then asked once more if the jar was full. The students responded with a unanimous "Yes." "Now," said the professor, "I want you to recognise that this jar represents your life.

"The stones are the important things – your family, your partner, your health, and your children – things that if everything else was lost and only they remained, your life would still be full.

"The pebbles are the other things that matter – like your job, your house, your car.

"The sand is everything else, the small stuff. If you put the sand into the jar first," he continued, "there is no room for the pebbles or the stones.

"The same goes for your life. If you spend all your time and energy on the small stuff, you will never have room for the things that are important to you.

"Pay attention to the things that are critical to your happiness.

"Play with your children.

"Take your partner out dancing.

"There will always be time to go to work, clean the house, give a dinner party, or fix the toilet. Take care of the rocks first – the things that really matter.

"Set your priorities. The rest is just sand."

Most people suffer from self-sabotage

OPEN

1. Is there anything you can admit now that it is your mistake?
2. What is emotional intelligence?

DIGEST

1. What is the most important thing in your life? How are you treating it? Why?
2. What is your biggest regret today?

RELATE

1. If you were to give advice on how to treat others like we wish to be treated, what would it be?

One of the deadliest failure-inducing attitudes we see today is to compete resentfully with others.

In my life, I have encountered people who literally pretended to like me, simply because they realised I was two times ahead of them.

All they wanted was to learn a thing or two and beat me at the game. They hated my guts. They hated my shadow. They hated my breath.

The unfortunate part is that a jealous man remains weak on the inside and deprived on the outside.

He suffers judgement and discrimination. He grapples with lack of progress in his life because he cares too much about the enemy and builds a shield to protect himself.

I always saw through my haters who would often team up with my associates in an attempt to discredit me. And I always upped my game to spite them. I would tell them about my plans and make them resent me even more, knowing that by so doing, I was delaying their own plans.

Here is the thing I have realised: when you are hated, people pay attention and try to find what your haters see in you. That is how your good works get glorified and recognised. Not being able to accept the things you can do is a serious self-sabotage. You will be like a loose cannon and go around ridiculing others. You even get paranoid and deride them in front of their confidants.

7 Important Life Lessons
You Should Never Forget

Gardner's Five Minds for the Future to Avoid Self-Sabotage

1. **The Disciplinary Mind:** make sure you know your thing, be it at work, school, in business or in partnership.

2. **The Synthesizing Mind:** the ability to integrate ideas from different disciplines or spheres into a coherent framework and to communicate that integration to others.

3. **The Creating Mind:** the capacity to uncover and clarify new problems, questions, and phenomena.

4. **The Respectful Mind:** awareness of and appreciation for differences among human beings and human groups.

5. **The Ethical Mind:** fulfilment of one's responsibilities as a worker and as a citizen.

Fifth Piece: The Important Things In Life

More than the problem, it's your reaction that creates chaos

At a restaurant, a cockroach suddenly flew from somewhere and landed on a lady.

She started screaming in fear.

With a panic-stricken face and trembling voice, she started jumping, both her hands desperately trying to get rid of the cockroach.

Her reaction was contagious, as everyone in her group also started panicking. The lady finally managed to push the cockroach away – but it landed on another lady in the group.

Now, it was the turn of the other lady in the group to continue the drama.

A waiter rushed forward to their rescue and the cockroach fell upon him. The waiter stood firm, composed himself and observed the behaviour of the cockroach on his shirt. When he was confident enough, he grabbed it with his fingers and threw it out of the restaurant.

Sipping my coffee and watching the drama, the antenna of my mind picked up a few thoughts and I began to wonder – was the cockroach responsible for their histrionic behaviour?

If so, then why was the waiter not disturbed? She handled it to near perfection, without any chaos. It was not the cockroach that disturbed the ladies, but the inability of those ladies to handle the disturbance.

I realised that, it is not the shouting of my father or my boss or my wife that disturbs me, but it's my inability to handle the disturbances caused by their shouting that disturbs me.

It's not the traffic jam on the road that disturbs me, but my inability to handle the effects of the traffic jam.

More than the problem, it's your reaction to the problem that creates chaos in your life.

A snake sheds off its skin but remains the same. So do human beings, they never change, they just never live to the fullest of their potential.

Life is a gift.

Today, before you think of saying an unkind word – think of someone who can't speak.

Before you complain about the taste of your food – think of someone who has nothing to eat.

Before you complain about your husband or wife – think of someone who is crying out to God for a companion.

Today before you complain about life – think of someone who went too early to heaven.

Before you complain about your children – think of someone who desires children but is barren.

Before you argue about who didn't clean your dirty house, – think of the people who live in the streets.

Before whining about the distance you drive – think of someone who walks the same distance with their feet.

And when you are tired and complain about your job – think of the unemployed, the disabled and those who wish they had your job.

But before you think of pointing the finger or condemning another – remember that not one of us is without sin and we all answer to one maker.

And when depressing thoughts seem to get you down – put a smile on your face and thank God you're alive and still around.

Life is like a camera...

Focus on what's important,

Capture the good times,

Develop from the negatives,

And if things don't work out,

Take another shot.

What to do when you do not know what you are doing

There are three types of people - those who know what they do, those who do not, and those who pretend as if they do.

Truth is that we don't necessarily have to have our lives figured out from the get go. Life is a process and there are flaws in every system.

The principle that society enforces on us that we should know it all about the future is a heaping pile of socially crafted gibberish that has been superimposed on our psyches since kindergarten, and it is holding us back.

The narrative that we should get our lives sorted from an early age killed many fervent dreamers.

Even after university education, one would still find it difficult to explain who they really are. Higher education institutions, at the very best, educate people for an occupation but do not educate (prepare) them for life.

That is the reason universities produce so many unemployed graduates and that is the reason life has produced the three kind of people mentioned above.

Let us learn life; it is the best teacher.

- You owe nothing to your younger self. It can't be perfect even if you fast for forty days.

- You are not responsible for being the person you once thought you'd be. Life happens.

- But you do owe something to the adult you are today. You cannot work on your yesterday, but today is the right moment to work on your tomorrow.

"Though no one can go back and make a brand new start, anyone can start from now and make a brand new ending." – Carl Bard.

People who know what they are doing are those curious fellows who always go beyond the call of average. To know what you are doing you have to be curious. Curiosity means you are eager to learn. When you are not curious, you get tempted to live a sweet lie when your friends make the best out of the chances and take an advantage of multiple opportunities they get.

Courage makes you push until something happens. It takes you to places where something is going to happen. What I love about pressure is that it is twofold – negative and positive. It bursts a pipe and it equally produces a diamond. Never succumb to pressure, use it to perfect your talents.

People who don't know what they are doing are often sensitive and less curious. They are always under negative pressure. They want their opinions to be validated by others. They normally do this when they happen to be superior in a group, whether by age or knowledge. You find that such a person is exposed to a certain thing and assumes others are less informed. In a group, they impose their ideas and want to take precedence.

Such people never learn. They remain in one level and fail to adapt to change. If you don't know something, stop justifying why you are wrong. Learn from others. Success comes from good habits. If you are not sure about what you are doing, always say less than unnecessary.

People who have pride are those who pretend like they know what they are doing. You find someone feeling embarrassed to seek assistance from others simply because they brag about being smart. They make people think they have everything under control. You get ashamed to look for help and always be the last to know about things and opportunities.

Such people lack confidence because they never try new things. I had a childhood friend who would not even do shopping during the day because he did not want to be seen as ordinary. He always made me carry a loaf of brown bread. But I did not mind, because my payment was eating with him. And I saved a lot of money. Today, life is hard for him. He is not as creative as he was supposed to be. He sabotaged himself.

7 Acts of Self-Sabotage

1. Always being angered by other people's success.

2. Talking disparagingly about others – especially to their friends.

3. Being emotionally defensive, taking every remark personally.

4. Competing unnecessarily for recognition.

5. Denial of the obvious, which makes you appear stupid.

6. Attempting to do everything and end up by displaying your flaws.

7. Always taking offence and feeling undermined without cause.

Sixth Piece

Entrepreneurship

Sixth Piece: Entrepreneurship

About the piece

*Purpose and problem, extremely contrasting as they are, often cut across the mind of today's young people as one and the same thing – perhaps because the symptoms are the same: determination, zest and something that **oils** inquisitiveness, urge and hunger.*

It has proven to be very dangerous, on several accounts, that confusing the two is not only unsafe, but excites unborn passions in most young people.

They are desperate to escape social ills such as financial slavery, uncertainty, lack and many other worries. That is why today 7 out of 10 young people have registered companies.

Unluckily or unfortunately, a nice company name does not translate into a successful business. The very same companies die before celebrating their first anniversary.

Some run at a deficit caused by bank charges while the owner waits for the first invoice or cheque— that is not coming. You find that some company founders don't even know what an annual return is, and as a result they fail to comply with Companies Act. However, I do not blame them: they are only trying to escape humble beginnings.

This chapter seeks to prepare the entrepreneurial mind to get started on some real business. Key to this chapter is preparing the reader, through realities of the cruel business world, to kick off a sound business with a solid business plan, real product and seductive marketing.

OPEN

1. How did you feel when doing multiplication at school?
2. When you see 9 what comes to your mind?

DIGEST

1. From the table on the right, what can you say about it?

RELATE

1. Have you ever felt like your life changed after getting a multiplication right? What happened?

Study the following pattern to stretch and electrify your mind. This chapter needs someone who is psychologically prepared, expressively ready, meaningfully committed, emotionally mature, physically brave, and tactically sharp.

What do you see and think about the following nine times table?

9 x 1	= 09
9 x 2	= 18
9 x 3	= 27
9 x 4	= 36
9 x 5	= 45
9 x 6	= 54
9 x 7	= 63
9 x 8	= 72
9 x 9	= 81
9 x 10	= 90

Now that you have thought about the above table. Let's agree to disagree that life is easier when you think fast and correctly.

The pattern has many interpretations. One may see, from the answers on the right, an **ASCENDING PATTERN** from 0 to 09 as initial numbers, like in **0**9, **1**8, **2**7. . .

*And another may see the opposite as in from 0 to 9 but using the last number in an **ASCENDING ORDER**, like 0, 1, 2 in 9**0**, 8**1**, 7**2** . . .*

*Yet another may see a **DESCENDING PATTERN** from 9 to 0 as last numbers, like 0**9**, 1**8**, 2**7** . . .*

*From the very same pattern, if you add the two numbers (totals) on the right, **YOU WILL ALWAYS GET 9**, as in 0 + 9, 1 + 8, 2 + 7 . . .*

*Amusingly, someone from the first five totals sees **THE REFLECTION OR MIRROR** of the last five totals, pairing the first and the last, like 09 and 90, 18 and 81, 27 and 72...*

The message in this rational workout is that a business is built on the foundation of seeing an ordinary thing in a different light.

I guess by now you are thinking of the first chapter, which talked about scrutinizing your situation and taking a different shape.

You do the same here, but now for the sake of making money, you are taking a giant leap.

Sixth Piece: Entrepreneurship

South Africa breeds Bloodsucking Hustlership

Whenever I hear these words from the government, "The youth must engage in entrepreneurship to beat unemployment" I feel like vomiting.

The reason South Africa is far from winning the fight against the tripartite challenges of poverty, unemployment and equality is because there are no systems in place to encourage and support entrepreneurship and fuel ground-breaking action.

Our young, so-called "business-minded", are in fact practising "parasitical approach" to entrepreneurship. Most of them do not come up with original ideas or aim to identify a niche area or gap in the market in their business plans. And frankly put, it is not a business if it doesn't provide a solution to a particular market.

This parasitical approach is fuelled by the government and its business agencies. For instance, SARS created self-service centres where businesses can obtain tender and good standing clearance, and whatever business certificates.

The service centres, centralised in Pretoria, rob off the capital of small, rural businesses as they have to pay at least a minimum of R350 for travelling.

That's why there are hundreds of businesses that charge the poor over R500 for free SARS papers. The system has created a new form of inequality that targets the most vulnerable people – people who do not have stable incomes.

Sadly, the economy could only grow and get off the ground on a supersonic speed if we create economic infrastructures that seek to promote entrepreneurship. But dololo.

It is because our government established development programmes that are based on racist Eurocentric ideologies, which were designed and championed by the colonisers who sought to perpetuate western imperialism.

These problematic models remain far removed from our social economic conditions. These happen because we have anti-intellectual government that ignores research and common sense when they develop policies.

They simply copy and imitate global trends without considering the uniqueness of our local needs and problems. Ideas, in these complex areas, could only succeed if they have been localised.

We cannot use foreign standards, which are usually glossed and sanitised through the language of free market economy, to measure our local progress and develop our economy.

We need to think carefully about our stands in the global economy. Benchmarking is dangerous when it is not domesticated. Good initiatives by government remain useless because they do not directly speak to our local challenges, such as lack of funds and access.

This is one complex example of the struggles our youth face. The system and pressures teach us to exploit our own.

The only Black business that seems to be thriving is a food business that is housed in a tavern - modern liquor restaurant or shisanyama.

And it is simply because drunkards and party animals increase by the day whereas entrepreneurship dies a natural death.

The arts and culture sector equally suffers exploitation. We see promoters who work so hard to organise events, but without reaping rewards for their sweats.

They tend to exploit their own artists under the pretence of exposing them to the real world. That is not business. It does not provide solution to the rural talented.

This problem is intersectional. It also hinges on the flaws of our education system which does not promote entrepreneurship. Even students who are studying business and entrepreneurship are not encouraged to come with their own ideas but to conform to the common notion of seeking employment.

The programme teaches them how to be effective business leaders, ethics, management theories, human resources etc. It does not teach them how to start their own businesses.

These graduates are taught to manage what is already there rather than creating. The curriculum is not useful. If the government believes in promoting entrepreneurship, they must inculcate its principles into the education system. But dololo.

Sixth Piece: Entrepreneurship

Maybe the following scenario can help some of you to start thinking out of tenders, manipulation, nepotism and corruption.

Lesego and Arthur joined a company together shortly after their graduation from university. After a few years of work, their manager promoted Arthur to a position of senior sales manager, but Lesego remained in his entry level as a junior sales officer.

Lesego became jealous and disgruntled, but continued working anyway.

One day he felt that he could not work with Arthur any more. He wrote his resignation letter, but before he submitted it to the manager, he complained that management did not value hard-working staff, but only promoted the favoured.

Therefore, in order to help him to realise this, the manager gave him a task. "Go and find out if anyone is selling water melons in town."

Lesego returned and said, "Yes, there is someone!"

The manager asked, "How much per kg?" He drove back to town to ask and then returned to inform the manager, "They are R13.50 per kg!"

The manager told him, "I will give Arthur the same task that I gave you."

So the manager said to Arthur, in the presence of Lesego: "Go and find out if anyone is selling water melons in town?"

He went to find out and on his return he said:

"Manager, there is only one person selling water melons in the whole town. The cost is R 49.00 for each water melon and R 32. 50 for a half melon. He sells them at R 13.50 per kg when sliced. He has in his stock 93 melons, each one weighing about 7kg. He has a farm and can supply us with melons

Sixth Piece: Entrepreneurship

for the next four months at a rate of 102 melons per day at R 27.00 per melon, this includes delivery.

The melons appear fresh and red with good quality, and they taste better than the ones we sold last year. He has his own slicing machine and is willing to slice for us free of charge. We need to strike a deal with him before 10am tomorrow and we will be sure of beating last year's profits in melons by R 223. This will contribute positively to our overall performance as it will add a minimum of 3.78% to our current overall sales target.

I have put this information down in writing and is available on spreadsheet. Please let me know if you need it as I can send it to you in fifteen minutes."

To be successful in life you must be observant, proactive and willing to do more, think more and holistically, have a more holistic perspective and go beyond the call of duty.

In short, this moral lesson summarises business. Lazy thinking is not allowed in business. I know a lot of people who think registering a company name is having a business. How sad! Successful businesses are those whose owners are more observant, think more and seek to gain an in-depth understanding of their niche areas. A successful person sees, and think about, the future and build an infrastructure and networks to attain his goals whole other indulge in narrow, short-sighted thinking.

Business requires strategy, which explains both long and short term plans as well as how the owner hopes to implement them. In that strategy, there should be everything the business needs. Generally, an average business person develops a five-year plan and works towards it. But he also must develop a contingency plan that hopes to capitalise on unexpected opportunities.

Sixth Piece: Entrepreneurship

Every Business Has an Imperfect Beginning

Stop waiting for the 'perfect' to happen; it is time to begin.

If you have read about the history of Tim Tebeila, you would know that he started by selling apples and bus tickets. By then he was at primary school, travelling more than 5km every day.

Today he stands firm as Limpopo's richest man.

But risks must be taken, because the greatest hazard in life is to risk nothing. The person who risks nothing, does nothing, has nothing and is nothing.

They may avoid suffering and sorrow but they cannot learn, feel, change, grow, love, live. Chained by their certitudes, they are a slaves, they have forfeited their freedom.

Only a person who risks is free.

Sixth Piece: Entrepreneurship

Start Up, Develop and Smile When Hard Work Pays Off

Like the woman in the Bible who had ten silver coins and lost one, she lit a lamp, swept the house and searched carefully until she found the coin. Your start-up is very important.

Same as one lost sheep in a hundred that Jesus went to search for, each asset you attach to your business adds value to the quality of the service you are going to provide.

If your business is in graphic designing and printing services, but you decide to use your only laptop to play computer games, and load it with materials such as music, movies, and pictures, it will attract viruses, become slower, and eventually crash.

And you will need to money to fix it.

If you don't fix it, people won't stand in long queues and will simply go next door. What I am saying is, value the little you have in order to have much more.

Every single cent of your business money counts. If you can have a mentality that a missing cent from a million reduces one from the status of being a millionaire, the better financial thinker you will become.

Business people who are rich today built their wealth from zero and knew how to husband their resources.

They knew how to husband every cent and used it to create their multimillion projects and investments.

The idea is to make money, and use the money to make more money. Use more money to make a legacy. And then use the legacy to inspire greatness in others.

These scenarios remain a distant possible for many people. It remains a fairy tale among hundreds of hopeful young people in South Africa who are wondering in the wilderness of unemployment.

Many open businesses because the National Development Plan (NDP) has influenced them. The plan remains vague and does not provide concrete strategies of leading the country, leaving many youth with vague ideas which inspire their desire to start their business. The situation is cloudy.

Firstly, these youngsters never learn anything about running a business – not even a financial background.

Some even think registering a business name is having a business. I am not sure if they are throwing themselves under the bus or the NDP is doing the throwing.

Seven in ten of those companies are deregistered by default every two months – because the owners did not even know that they had to file annual returns every financial year-end.

Failure to do so results in the Commission (CICP) assuming that the company and/or close corporation is not doing business or is not intending on doing business in the near future.

Many of the small businesses do not have any prospect or original idea. The owners are secretively self-appointed, and are agencies or middlemen who pretend to be offering certain services.

That is why their services are always unreliable and of poor quality. No wonder they are always taken to Speak Out for failing to deliver either on time or nothing at all.

Interestingly, these small businesses contribute to 40% of the Gross Domestic Product (GDP) but are not sustainable. Which results in a loss of about 80% of jobs created.

Some businesses which do not work as middlemen also suffer closure within five years. This is because the owners do not have sound business plans and lack financial skills as well as marketing.

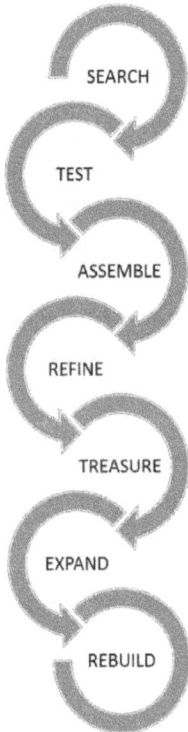

The STARTER Model

SEARCH

TEST

ASSEMBLE

REFINE

TREASURE

EXPAND

REBUILD

This STARTER Model serves as a seven-step pointer for the hopeful entrepreneur to escape their torments and to move their businesses in the right direction. Seven out of ten businesses, or should I say business ideas, do not have business plans. The following model was drafted after I have sampled thirty (30) small businesses owned by youth between the ages of 20 and 35 in Limpopo and Northern Cape Provinces, where poverty is beyond the tipping point. Through participant observation, drafted the model as a quick guide to developing a sound business.

1. **SEARCH** for a need in the market and do research about it. You should have a clear business idea and an area of business. At this stage, your entrepreneurial needs should guide you to conduct a SWOT analysis and derive at business objectives, mission and vision.

2. **TEST** your idea by doing a basic viability study. This stage, although premature, should be more strategic than tactical. Find out which areas of your plan will not work and which areas will need more focus and further development. As you get feedback, identify and discard what may be impractical and impossible to achieve from your initial idea and remain with what will bring in money.

3. **ASSEMBLE** resources informed by the testing process. In this phase, you know what needs to be done. You start putting together resources that enable sales for the first year or first few months. You already know how much you will need to service a certain number of clients.

4. **REFINE** your plan based on your experiences and further research. Experience is the best teacher. When your business starts operating, it always involves some risk. This will help you to sharpen the service for improved quality and enable you to secure distribution and marketing.

5. **TREASURE** your business. There is no better marketing than embracing, selling and living the idea. At this stage, you should start taking the business out to the world and exposing it to competition and more challenges as your clientele grows. This

is where you meet at gala dinners, business seminars and open days.

6. **EXPAND** your business. The more people know about your services, the better the portfolio. Opportunities start opening up, giving room for growth. At this stage, the entrepreneur should go back to the initial plan and revive and refine the he considered impossible at the TESTING stage.

7. **REBUILD** the business and broaden the vision. The planning cycle is a continuous process. As you do more research you will change your thinking and strategy, which will, in turn, inform further research and new business development. No wonder companies keep on changing tag lines (slogans) – today it's *Simpler, Better, Faster* and tomorrow is *Moving Forward*. Now you know the reason.

That's how it goes. This model is a quick guide to business planning. During the study of the behaviour and trends of small businesses, I have also noticed that the owners confused a business plan with a business profile.

The following section will draw an unfading, bold line between the two. As I said, many people have business ideas, but it takes planning to make the idea functional.

That's precisely why, if you intend to build a business from your idea, it's helpful to create a business plan. It will enable you to build and refine your concept, showing you its potential and failure, both logistically and financially.

From the business plan, you will summarise it and form what we call a business profile - a portfolio of evidence that targets a particular business or project. It is more like a quote.

Business Plan vs. Business Profile

A business plan documents the vision for your business and how you intend to achieve that it. It contains financial projections of what the business will cost to develop and operate, plus an estimation of the revenues to be generated.

Its purpose is to provide a detailed explanation of your business to give potential investors, suppliers, prospective employees, accountants etc. some indications of how your business is going to work.

A profile is limited in scope and generally has a specific audience. The primary reason for a business profile is to solicit or develop a business opportunity.

It is a quick description of your company's services and products and work done before as quality assurance.

In simple terms, having a business profile without a business plan is like drinking water when you are hungry. It only impresses but cannot secure a great business deal.

It introduces your business but does not focus on what makes you different and how the difference will be sustained. But a business plan does.

Your Network is Your Net Worth

This section is tied to the previous piece on mentorship, under the section about receiving favour.

Favour in this context, as I said before, is not foul play or nepotism but the trust that one is capable of doing something.

Your network here is exactly what you are going to take home in business, net pay.

Funnel of Benefits from Networking

Generation of Referrals
Increased Confidence
Raising Your Profile
Shared Knowledge
Opportunities
Connections
Learning
Advice

Seventh Piece

God Is Your Success

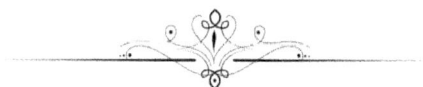

Seventh Piece: God Is Your Success

About the Piece

OPEN

1. Are you happy with your work, be it school, working place or artistically?

DIGEST

1. What do you think constitutes excellence?

RELATE

1. Have you ever felt like you have been excellent at your work but not recognised? What

God's grace is sufficient for you. Often God places his blessings in the valley of worry, distress, disappointment, and impossibility. Many people give up on their dreams, hopes, aspirations, and purpose because they do not want to face the giant in front of them. Some face the unemployment giant and some the under-employment giant. Some have their loved ones addicted to drugs. Some are troubled by unfaithful partners. Whatever the case, never think there is someone who will stand up to your problems. All you have to do is be prepared to fight your own battles. Preparation means choosing the right weapons. Your greatest weapon is God. God is your success. This chapter helps you to get rid of anything that doesn't work for you. It teaches you perseverance and bravery. The key message is to understand the rewards of winning. It instils in you the stamina to do something with what is in your hand. Do what you can, with what you have, where you are. God uses challenges to reveal our true blessings, to uncover our purpose and get rid of your enemies. Face your challenges. Enjoy the rewards. The most imperative thing to remember, in any challenge, is that you have already won in the blood of Jesus. You are already a victor, the trial is just your way to claim your prize. Triumph is certain when you partner with God.

God Blesses Excellence

And we know that in all things God works for the good of those who love him, who have been called according to his purpose
— Romans 8:28

At one team building session, I requested a one-on-one session with the employees to find out about their habits. I wanted to know about their organisational culture, not according to policy but personalities. I did the same with a few more companies.

I have realised that in many organisations, employees get to work late.

You get to work at 08h00 and start by making coffee. One company even had a tea society. At around 9h30 they are done with coffee and start making a few of personal calls.

Typically, each employee started working at around 10h00. And went for an official tea break at 11h00, typically working half a day every day.

And I told them that God rewards excellence. Their behaviour was standing against their promotion. But being excellent does not mean you are perfect. It means you pay attention to detail and do the right thing.

Being excellent simply means one improves every day. Some people wonder why they don't get promotion, not knowing that their line managers were watching.

Thomas Edison tried two thousand different materials in search of a filament for the light bulb. When none of strategies worked, his assistant started complaining: "All our work is in vain. We have learned nothing." Edison replied very confidently: "Oh, we have come a long way and we have learned a lot. We know that there are two thousand elements which we cannot use to make a good light bulb." Now that element number two thousand and one was the right one, God blessed it so it can live longer and benefit the generations to come. Even today people find it hard to live without a bulb.

If you are at the same level, you don't improve at your work, you will never get promoted. Look for a mentor and learn new skills. You should not be at the same level for more than a year. Look for ways that you will improve and reach your highest potential.

Excellence is a result of learning new things daily. To learn new things, you have to move on and stop moving around. Your comfort zone does not hold any excellence. We excel when we meet new challenges.

We are all made to fly — to realise our incredible potential as human beings. But at times we sit on our branches, clinging to the things that are familiar to us. The possibilities are endless, but for most of us, they remain undiscovered. We conform to the familiar, the comfortable, and the mundane. So for the most part, our lives are mediocre instead of exciting, thrilling and fulfilling. Let us learn to destroy the branch of fear we cling to and free ourselves to the glory of flight!

God Is On Time

Patience is not the ability to wait, but how you act while you're waiting.

Just like everyone has the knowledge that the Son will come. The day is not known. How you wait for Him is what matters more than how long is He going to take.

For when He comes, he is going to look only for those who deserve a place in His kingdom. God is good all the time, all the time God is good! His eyes are not blind to our struggles nor His ears deaf to our cries.

God promised the Israelites freedom from Egypt. The Lord had given them the promise that one day they would be freed from slavery and taken to the Promised Land.

However, when they faced opposition and were not freed exactly when they thought they would be, they lost hope of the Lord's deliverance altogether.

Getting discouraged and refusing to listen to God's word any more is the most dangerous part about waiting.

Be still. God works behind the scenes. You will not see him in action every day, but you will eventually see His progress in your life when you least expect it.

"Not a single one of all the good promises the Lord had given to the family of Israel was left unfulfilled; everything he had spoken came true." – Joshua 21:45

Many people miss their blessings because they do not work on time.

Time does not just come to you, but you have to fight for it.

Ten virgins took their lamps and went out to meet the bridegroom. The foolish five, who did not carry extra oil the door was shut in their absence. They could not get to what they were waiting for, what they worked hard for, and what they hoped for. It is because they thought God's time is their time.

Many people become impatient or do not see it through to the end of time because they do not wait upon the Lord; they allocate time to the Lord. God's timing is perfect. He is always on time and on point.

We human miss Him because we are late or too early. All you have to do is to keep on watching, because you do not know when your time will come.

There is a season for each one of us. Wait for your season and do not mind the season of others.

Sometimes we squander our blessings because we push God to give them to us before the actual time. Like the prodigal son who asked his father to give him his share of the estate.

God knows what is good for you and at what time. Your promotion is coming, continue doing your best. Your prize is ahead, continue running your race.

5 Ps of Success

Moruntrac Model

*This model views life as a race that starts when one receives knowledge and has no finishing line. Whether sprinting, jogging or walking, the runners get compensated after the completion of each and every lap. Moruntrac Model, derived from **Mor**eroa's **Unt**imed **Rac**e, helps people understand their life journey and appreciate that every step of life prepares one for the greatness ahead.*

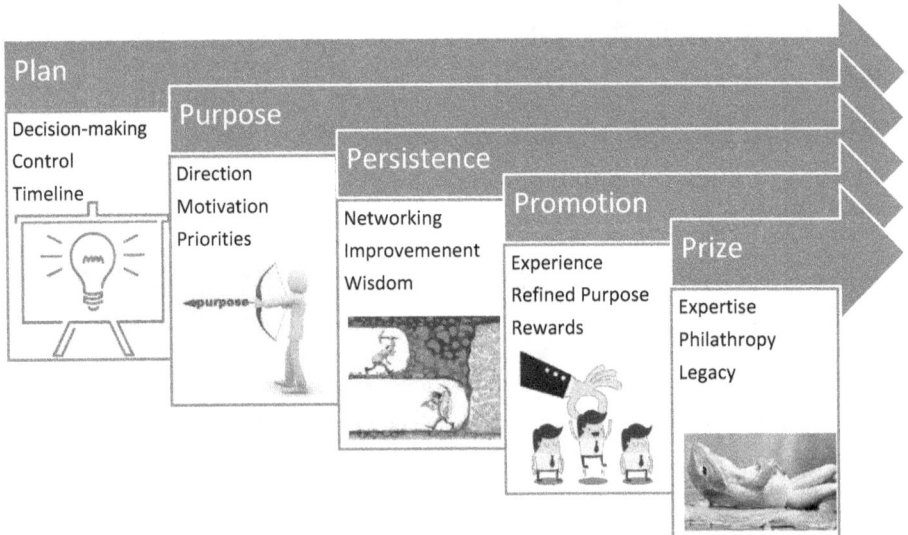

Plan
Decision-making
Control
Timeline

Purpose
Direction
Motivation
Priorities

purpose

Persistence
Networking
Improvemenent
Wisdom

Promotion
Experience
Refined Purpose
Rewards

Prize
Expertise
Philathropy
Legacy

In this model, I plan to make your life look a bit better. We should stop living aimlessly and spontaneously. There are people who live unintended lives because they did not plan their lives.

Planning your life is simply taking a decision that certain things will stay and others will leave your life. That is simply taking control of your situation and use it empower yourself. Everything that needs control has time.

If you want to achieve a certain goal, give it a season as some goals cannot be achieved in a particular season. Although life has expectations, against all unforeseen circumstances, you will never be quite far from where you expected to be, should things not go according to your plan. This is unlike not knowing how far or close your dream is.

Plan gives one a purpose in life. When you set timelines, it becomes easy for you to have direction.

You know what to do and for how long. This is, in itself, a motivation to keep seeking the best out of your sweat. You would not want to invest in things that would not contribute to your purpose. Hence, direction motivates one to set their priorities straight.

People with a detailed plan often shoot straight to their life purpose.

But purpose alone is not enough. It should arise passion and give one courage to continue even when everything stops. Sometimes life support stops, friends disappear, favour ceases, and hope fades away.

To be persistent, you have to associate continuously with people who will steer your goal to new levels. Networking often serves as a gauge that one is making strides. Through other people we are able to learn new things and improve. There is no other wisdom than learning life from others.

Most people, who now enjoy fruits of being at the top, were promoted by wisdom – the ability to associate with the right people and use them as their corrections, developments and forewarnings.

A well-thought-out life plan encourages the individual to be persistent, as they know what needs to be done to reach the destination.

Persistence is always rewarded with promotion. You only move to the next level when you get through with the current level. Being at a particular level brews experience that you will need to start the next level.

Once you are experience, you ought to revise your life plan to aim even higher, as things become clearer and more realistic. Rewards are inevitable for people who stick to plan.

When you start getting recognised and rewarded for achieving your purpose or life plan, you become an expert in whatever area your plan was based in.

An expert is an achiever and superior. This is the right time to give back to the community through knowledge transfer and other community services. That's how legacy is built. That's living a life that matters.

Do the Right Thing Even When Nobody Is Watching

One day, when I was shopping for groceries at a supermarket in South Africa, I saw a well-dressed woman.

She picked up fresh milk, a cake from the bakery section, some vegetables and a toy, probably for her son because it was a truck. She then went to the section for rice and its seven colours.

She took the cake out of the basket and put it next to the rice. She then chose a type of rice.

The woman went on to take toiletries and decided that she did not need the milk any more, and left the milk where she was – in the lavatory section.

On the outside, she looked wonderful and perfect, but you could see through her actions that on the inside there was disorder, obstruction, exasperation and carelessness.

Her excellence was only on the outside. Just like a driver who knows very well that it is an offence not to wear a safety belt but never wears it.

When he sees traffic cops, he quickly fastens the belt. This is a serious disorder and disturbs progress.

God is always watching, we are only fooling ourselves.

The Double 7 Golden Rules of Living A Happy Life – The If Model

If you open it, close it.

If you turn it on, turn it off.

If you unlock it, lock it up.

If you break it, admit it.

If you can't fix it, call in someone who can.

If you borrow it, return it.

If you value it, take care of it.

If you make a mess, clean it up.

If you move it, put it back.

If you don't know how to operate it, leave it alone.

If it's none of your business, don't ask questions.

If it isn't broke, don't fix it.

If it will brighten someone's day, say it.

If it will tarnish someone's reputation, keep it to yourself.

Turn Your Challenges Upside Down

Your life may look like this image: ugly, depressed, unattractive, and unpleasant.

*But **TURN THIS PAGE UPSIDE DOWN** and see that there is hope on the other side.*

Life obstacles are like a seed that germinates from the soil. For a seed to sprout, it has to go through pressure and uncertainty. When seeds are planted, they first grow roots.

Once the roots take hold, a small plant will begin to emerge and eventually break through the soil. If there is a hard surface or a rock – or obstacle – that the seed can't handle, it takes a new direction.

As the plant begins to make its own food from nutrients it takes from the soil, it grows bigger.

We face difficult hardships in life which sometimes make us feel like throwing in the towel. That is like a seed when it is thrown underground.

Like a small seed that has to spring out of the ground, we learn to find our stronghold through the sufferings. Despite their small size, though, seeds contain food and all the instructions necessary to sprout to life as a plant.

We also have to face our challenges, be consistent (grow roots), push forward for our ability to come out of a challenge strong holds solutions to hundreds of people around us.

The solutions to life problems are definitely taken from the problem itself. That is why the tree takes nutrients from the soil. The solution comes from within. The challenges we face are not there to harm us but teach us lessons.

We learn various ways of solving our problems in different circumstances. Like a plant that faces a rock on its way to the top.

Sometimes we become familiar with pain and uncertainty to such an extent that we get used to our fears and worries. And, as a result, we never see opportunities in the midst of those challenges.

Do not let obstacles scare you off. Samson could not allow a roaring lion coming towards him to end his journey to Timnah. He faced the lion and tore it apart with his bare hands.

You do not need so many materials or tools to get started with your dreams, or continue with your purpose.

David could not have defeated Goliath if he wanted all the tools. Sometimes it is the tools that are too heavy for us to handle.

In Timnah, Samson found a wife. He had to use the same route to go back to marry the woman. Imagine if he turned away when the lion approached him. He could not have gotten what he wanted.

From the lion's carcass, there was a swarm of bees and honey. He took the honey and ate as he went along to marry the woman.

His blessings were placed in a lion.

> You could have heard him happily say, "Out of the eater, something to eat; out of the strong, something sweet."

This means that he did not know that from the lion, which is brutal and strong, would come the sweetness. But it had to die first, like a seed underground.

You need to remove your obstacles to build up your future. There are times in our lives when we are hit by blow after blow, and we feel crushed, exhausted and shuttered.

But God never wants us to live without courage, hope and belief. That is why He placed His power upon belief. It is only natural to have battles to fight every day. Struggles to go through, whether psychological, financial, physical or otherwise.

Never succumb to feelings of defeat. God knows what we can handle.

In Matthew, He says what seems impossible to men is possible to God. He can never give us a challenge that will defeat us.

Samson was prepared because the journey was long, and he needed to eat.

Success is a Result of Test

There was a man who had everything anybody else could have wished for: money, wealth, health, and a beautiful family. Tragedy struck him and he lost his wealth. Next, a storm took the lives of all his children. Then, a devastating disease left his body in excruciating pain.

Did Job have a bad moment and think of himself as a failure? Yes, and his wife also told him he was a loser. Like a test at school, whether you know the correct answers or not, in the middle of the test, you get tired, eyes swollen, the body weakens and mind exhausted.

But it is not the process of the test that will set you free, it is the result that will give you peace of mind. You might think you will not make it. You might want to quit. You might get discouraged. You happen to feel miserable. But the courage and purpose of life push you to continue. In discomfort we often find purpose. Healing comes when you get your mind off the difficulty you are going through.

Job regained everything he ever lost. Shame Satan and continue with your purpose.

Joseph, at 17 years, was miserable when his brothers misinterpreted his dreams. Sometimes we go through difficulty or the test of life because we are different from others. His brothers' anger and envy made them sell him into slavery.

Joseph was in this trouble, or test, not because he had committed any sin or mistake. Some of us lose our cool when people accuse or belittle us. Many times we seek revenge for we have been put through a lot by others. We develop anger for we don't know the purpose in the pain we are going through. If you only focus on the pain, you get negative. But often after the pain comes a great thing. Our purpose is covered in hardships.

Makwena Makgakga is today's favourite radio personality, who lost a job at a community station at one point. He was a good presenter. He had to stay jobless at home. But the pain prepared him to give birth to greatness. Your pain should inspire you to look for opportunities.

If he sat down and thought he was not good enough, he would not have tried something bigger than what he had lost. Today, he appears on TV mentoring innovative young South African. He is giving them access to their full potential. He is listened by over 3 million people, every day but he was dismissed from a listenership of less than 20 000.

Neither did Joseph fail.

He went on to become the wisest person during his time. He ruled and never took revenge on those who put him through the pain. He served them.

That is what purpose is all about, it is greater than your pain, pride, and greater than your future. Once you find your purpose, you will realise it is greater than you and cannot be contained within you. It will inspire greatness in others.

One might ask how to find the right path. Well, you never know it is the right path until you move and find what you are looking for. There is never the right or wrong path. The right path is hard work towards what is important to you. The wrong path is laziness and discouragement.

A master was strolling through a field of wheat when a disciple came up to him and asked, "I can't tell which the true path is. What's the secret?"

"What does that ring on your right hand mean?" asked the master.

"My father gave it to me before dying."

"Well, give it to me."

The disciple obeyed, and the master tossed the ring into the middle of the field of wheat.

"Now what?" shouted the disciple. "Now I have to stop doing everything I was doing to look for the ring! It's important to me!"

"When you find it, remember this: You yourself answered the question you asked me. That is how you tell the true path: It is more important than all the rest."

Partner with God

"For I know the plans I have for you," declares the LORD, "plans to prosper you and not to harm you, plans to give you hope and a future – Jeremiah 29:11

7 WAYS TO FIGHT STRESS BY HELPING YOURSELF

1. **Do not hold grudges:** It is not easy to see people who wronged you being happy. After what they have put you through, screwed you at work, embarrassed you in public, or caused your financial crisis. But holding onto these feelings has been proven to hurt physical and psychological health. Grudge ages you. Bitter people have high blood pressure. It weakens you. A grudge often has a spill over effect; it extends to hurt other people.

2. **Forgive:** Forgive and see it as something you are doing for you, not the person who wronged you. Let go. Forgiving is not reconciling, it does not mean you are giving a second time to those who hurt you. You just let it go. You will attain peace.

3. **Forget Perfection:** Stress is often a result of expectations we have of others, but most importantly ourselves. Never be obsessed with perfection to an extent that if you cannot get or do something you become stressed. No one is perfect. Practice makes perfect.

4. **Lighten Up:** Your stress levels are controlled by your mood. Sometimes we catch stress simply because we do not   have

happiness. Watch less serious films or read novels to ease your thoughts.

5. **Limit Emotional Involvement:** Most stressed people invested their time in things that do not matter that much. Wasting time is the most painful feeling ever. Never waste your time.

6. **Think Differently:** A remedy to controlling stress is to think differently about the things that stress you out. As simple as that.

7. **Accept your situation.**

The trick here is that stress is a thought. No more, no less. Exactly that. We have complete control over stress, because it's not something that happens to us but something that happens in us.

Yes, stress is bodily or mental tension resulting from factors that bother you. It might be a cheating partner, increasing financial responsibilities, studies or a wayward child. But it is all your thoughts out of balance.

To balance your thoughts, you need to know that some things happen in your life naturally, and you have to let time heal them. How you view the situation is the most important thing.

I suggest you partner with God. Do not hold on to stress and things you can't control. Change how you see those things. Better read the Bible more often than thinking about your worries.

A psychologist walked around a room while teaching stress management to an audience. As she raised a glass of water, everyone expected they'd be asked the "half empty or half full" question like I did in the first chapter. Instead, with a smile on her face, she inquired: "How heavy is this glass of water?"

Answers called out by the audience ranged from small to large numbers.

She replied, "The absolute weight doesn't matter. It depends on how long I hold it. If I hold it for a minute, it's not a problem. If I hold it for an hour, I will have an ache in my arm.

If I hold it for a day, my arm will feel numb and paralysed. In each case, the weight of the glass doesn't change, but the longer I hold it, the heavier it becomes."

The stresses and worries in life are like that glass of water. Think about them for a while and nothing happens. Think about them a bit longer and they begin to hurt. And if you think about them all day long, you will feel paralysed – incapable of doing anything.

It's important to remember to let go of your stresses. As early in the evening as you can, put all your burdens down. Don't carry them through the evening and into the night. Remember to put the glass down!

Partnering with God is exactly what Jesus explained in Matthew 6: 25:

Do not worry about your life, what you will eat or drink; or about your body, what you will wear. Is not life more than food, and the body more than clothes?

Look at the birds of the air; they do not sow or reap or store away in barns, and yet your heavenly Father feeds them. Are you not much more valuable than they? Can any one of you by worrying add a single hour to your life?

Surrender your problems to God. Stress will only kill you. Partner with God.

7 Signs That You've Partnered With God:

1. You feel completely lost and alone, sometimes stupid.

2. Your life feels false.

3. You crave for meaning and purpose.

4. You want more privacy.

5. You care less about the perceptions of society.

6. You're experiencing more synchronicity.

7. You feel deeper compassion and empathy towards others.

About the Author

His urbane personality and suave demeanour, as well as his sartorial elegance, always draw attention from people who meet MOSES MASHWAHLA MOREROA for the first time, but he insists that focusing on one's character and physical appearance could reduce the significance of their worth.

Nonetheless, Moses cut an audacious figure and has enjoyed the status of a child prodigy since he broke onto the public scene as an aspirational public speaker who is known for his oratory skills, wordplay, and wisdom.

Moses's rise to the podium defies all logical thinking and his understanding of spiritual growth and the significance of formal education in harnessing an individual's gifts secures him a seat among an elite of young leaders of his time.

Onlookers, including professors, graduates, and business people, would watch with awe and marvellous at his deep yet clear voice as the prodigy aced his role as the master of ceremonies at the University of Limpopo's graduation ceremony.

Moses wears many hats: He is a business and life coach, mentor, facilitator, and speaker. Home at writing, and strategic planning and thinking, he uses his gifts, experience to shape, and transform the profession of communication, business, and community development. With a career spanning close to a decade, Moses' public relations work has been recognised by the Public Relations Institute of Southern Africa (PRISA).

About The Author

He specialises in social media marketing and campaigning, and strategic planning. With seven years' experience in corporate communication and brand positioning.

Over the years, he has been engaged in team building and leadership development programmes. He is also an editor of note with footprints in professional editing for corporates, books, academic papers, integrated reports and social media campaigns.

He has trained hundreds of people in business, media and communication, and brand essence. For the last twelve years, he has been preaching the Good News, encouraging people to overcome their adversities and reach their full potential.

A Highway Africa and UNICEF scholar, Moses has interests in social media and communication for corporates, change management, and content marketing. He is an MBA candidate at the University of South Wales in the UK.

An educator, he currently plies his trades as a communicator at the University of Limpopo where he obtained Media and Communication, and PGCE qualifications.

He also holds a Certificate in Creative Writing, with distinction, from the UK Writers' College as well as International Computer Driving License, a Diploma in Business Management, and certificates in photography, radio and television production, graphic design, strategic management, public-private partnership, and leadership.

He was bred in a humble village called Segwashi, Ga-Mamabolo in Limpopo.

Professional Services:

- Speaking and Corporate MC
- Team Building and Auctioning Services
- Life Coach and Motivational Services
- Business Consulting and Planning

Tel: 081 284 9339 I Email: moses.moreroa@live.com

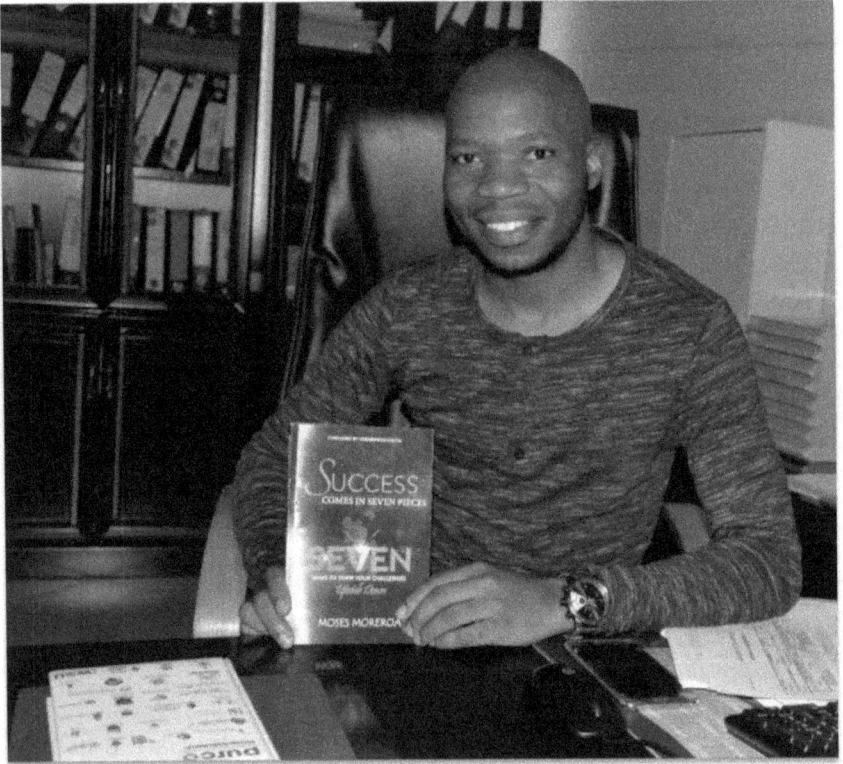

Additional Resources

http://academictips.org

HOLY BIBLE. *YouVersion Bible App, Version 7.4.4*

https://www.forbesafrica.com

Washington, Omer B. *I've learned*

Howard Gardner. *Five Minds for the Future*

Notes